Spring-clean those Maths skills with CGP!

Blow away the winter cobwebs with this CGP Daily Practice Book — it'll help pupils' Maths skills sparkle in the spring sunshine!

There's a page of brilliant Maths practice for every school day of the spring term, all covering vital skills from the Year 6 curriculum.

It's perfect for use in class or at home, with plenty of examples and splashes of colour to keep things interesting. Bring on spring!

What CGP is all about

Our sole aim here at CGP is to produce the highest quality books — carefully written, immaculately presented and dangerously close to being funny.

Then we work our socks off to get them out to you — at the cheapest possible prices.

Contents

☑ Use the tick boxes to help keep a record of which tests have been attempted.

Week 1
☑ Day 1 1
☑ Day 2 2
☑ Day 3 3
☑ Day 4 4
☑ Day 5 5

Week 2
☑ Day 1 6
☑ Day 2 7
☑ Day 3 8
☑ Day 4 9
☑ Day 5 10

Week 3
☑ Day 1 11
☑ Day 2 12
☑ Day 3 13
☑ Day 4 14
☑ Day 5 15

Week 4
☑ Day 1 16
☑ Day 2 17
☑ Day 3 18
☑ Day 4 19
☑ Day 5 20

Week 5
☑ Day 1 21
☑ Day 2 22
☑ Day 3 23
☑ Day 4 24
☑ Day 5 25

Week 6
☑ Day 1 26
☑ Day 2 27
☑ Day 3 28
☑ Day 4 29
☑ Day 5 30

Week 7
☑ Day 1 31
☑ Day 2 32
☑ Day 3 33
☑ Day 4 34
☑ Day 5 35

Week 8
☑ Day 1 36
☑ Day 2 37
☑ Day 3 38
☑ Day 4 39
☑ Day 5 40

Week 9
- [x] Day 1 41
- [x] Day 2 42
- [x] Day 3 43
- [x] Day 4 44
- [x] Day 5 45

Week 10
- [x] Day 1 46
- [x] Day 2 47
- [x] Day 3 48
- [x] Day 4 49
- [x] Day 5 50

Week 11
- [x] Day 1 51
- [x] Day 2 52
- [x] Day 3 53
- [x] Day 4 54
- [x] Day 5 55

Week 12
- [x] Day 1 56
- [x] Day 2 57
- [x] Day 3 58
- [x] Day 4 59
- [x] Day 5 60

Answers 61

Published by CGP

ISBN: 978 1 78908 659 1

Editors: Emily Forsberg, Emily Garrett, Josie Gilbert, Rob Hayman
With thanks to Glenn Rogers and Clare Selway for the proofreading.
With thanks to Lottie Edwards for the copyright research.

Clipart from Corel®

Printed by Elanders Ltd, Newcastle upon Tyne.
Based on the classic CGP style created by Richard Parsons.

Text, design, layout and original illustrations © Coordination Group Publications Ltd. (CGP) 2020
All rights reserved.

Photocopying this book is not permitted, even if you have a CLA licence.
Extra copies are available from CGP with next day delivery • 0800 1712 712 • www.cgpbooks.co.uk

How to Use this Book

- This book contains 60 daily practice tests.

- We've split them into 12 sections — that's roughly one for each week of the Year 6 spring term.

- Each week is made up of 5 tests, so there's one for every school day of the term (Monday – Friday).

- Each test should take about 10 minutes to complete.

- The tests contain a mix of topics from Year 6 Maths. New Year 6 topics are gradually introduced as you go through the book.

- The tests increase in difficulty as you progress through the term.

- Each test looks something like this:

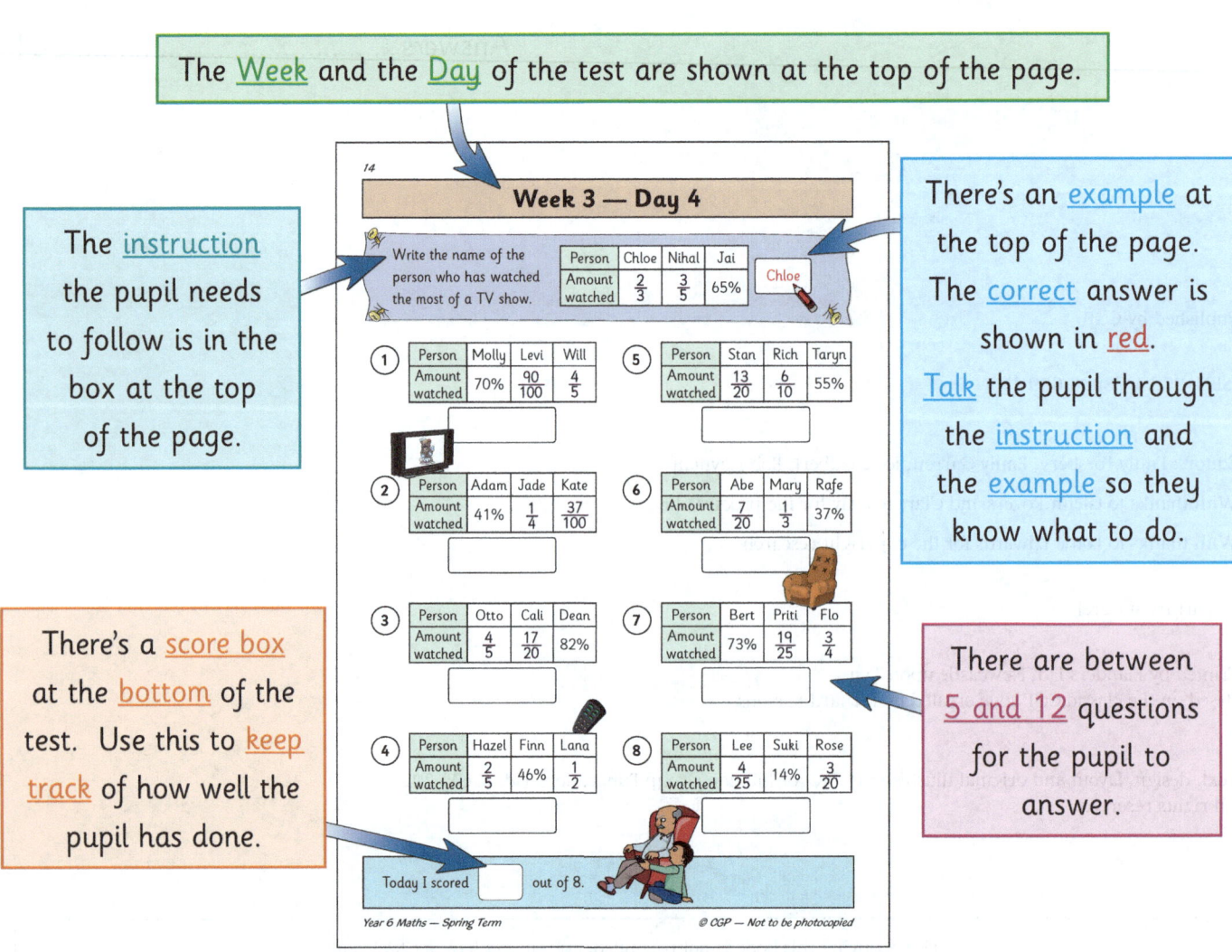

The Week and the Day of the test are shown at the top of the page.

The instruction the pupil needs to follow is in the box at the top of the page.

There's an example at the top of the page. The correct answer is shown in red. Talk the pupil through the instruction and the example so they know what to do.

There's a score box at the bottom of the test. Use this to keep track of how well the pupil has done.

There are between 5 and 12 questions for the pupil to answer.

Week 1 — Day 1

Alice digs a hole and Chris builds a tower. What is the difference in their heights?

Alice	−11 cm
Chris	34 cm

45 cm

1)
Alice	−25 cm
Chris	31 cm

____ cm

2)
Alice	−43 cm
Chris	27 cm

____ cm

3)
Alice	−17 cm
Chris	42 cm

____ cm

4)
Alice	−34 cm
Chris	26 cm

____ cm

5)
Alice	−9 cm
Chris	38 cm

____ cm

6)
Alice	−14 cm
Chris	55 cm

____ cm

7)
Alice	−28 cm
Chris	63 cm

____ cm

8)
Alice	−31 cm
Chris	46 cm

____ cm

9)
Alice	−47 cm
Chris	58 cm

____ cm

10)
Alice	−19 cm
Chris	74 cm

____ cm

11)
Alice	−37 cm
Chris	55 cm

____ cm

12)
Alice	−27 cm
Chris	89 cm

____ cm

Today I scored ____ out of 12.

Week 1 — Day 2

Write the answer in its simplest form. $\frac{2}{10} \times \frac{5}{7} = \frac{1}{7}$

1) $\frac{4}{5} \times \frac{1}{6} =$ ☐

2) $\frac{2}{3} \times \frac{1}{4} =$ ☐

3) $\frac{7}{12} \times \frac{3}{7} =$ ☐

4) $\frac{3}{12} \times \frac{2}{5} =$ ☐

5) $\frac{3}{4} \times \frac{5}{11} =$ ☐

6) $\frac{3}{10} \times \frac{6}{7} =$ ☐

7) $\frac{1}{6} \times \frac{3}{4} =$ ☐

8) $\frac{6}{8} \times \frac{7}{8} =$ ☐

9) $\frac{3}{5} \times \frac{4}{6} =$ ☐

10) $\frac{4}{8} \times \frac{5}{12} =$ ☐

11) $\frac{7}{10} \times \frac{4}{7} =$ ☐

12) $\frac{8}{12} \times \frac{3}{10} =$ ☐

Today I scored ☐ out of 12.

Week 1 — Day 3

How many visitors does the fair get in total?

3375 visitors every day for 29 days

97 875

$$\begin{array}{r} 3\,3\,7\,5 \\ \times2\,9 \\ \hline 3\,0_3\,3_6\,7_4\,5 \\ 6\,7_1\,5_1\,0\,0 \\ \hline 9\,7\,8\,7\,5 \end{array}$$

① 2143 visitors every day for 13 days

④ 4629 visitors every day for 72 days

② 6351 visitors every day for 34 days

⑤ 3276 visitors every day for 45 days

③ 9638 visitors every day for 18 days

⑥ 5285 visitors every day for 96 days

Today I scored [ ] out of 6.

Week 1 — Day 4

The average temperatures of two countries were measured during a week. What was the biggest temperature difference between the countries during this time?

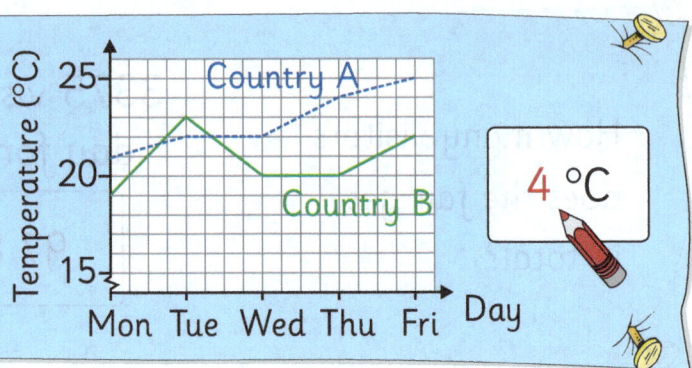

4 °C

1. ____ °C

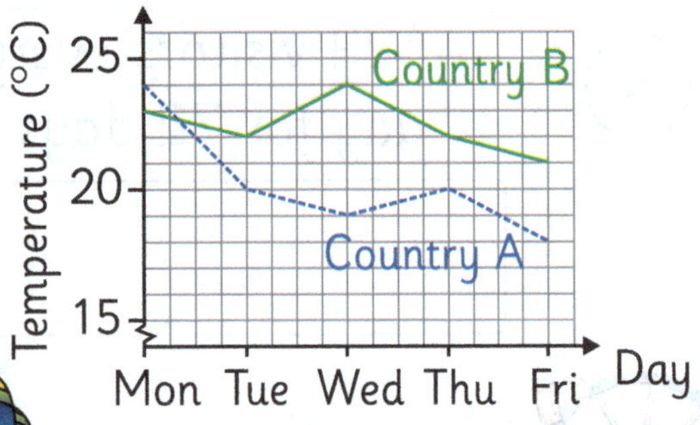

2. ____ °C

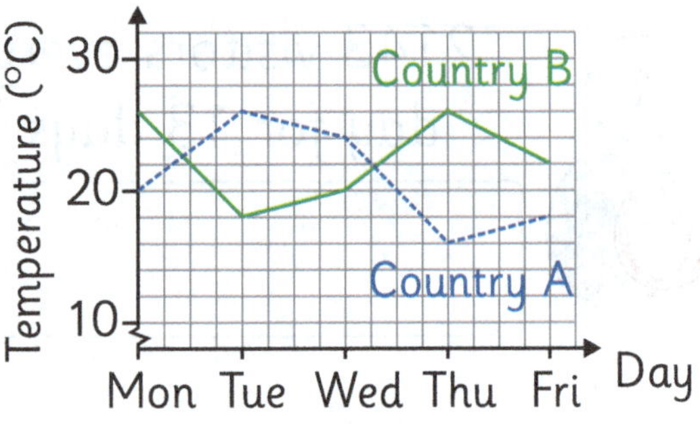

3. ____ °C

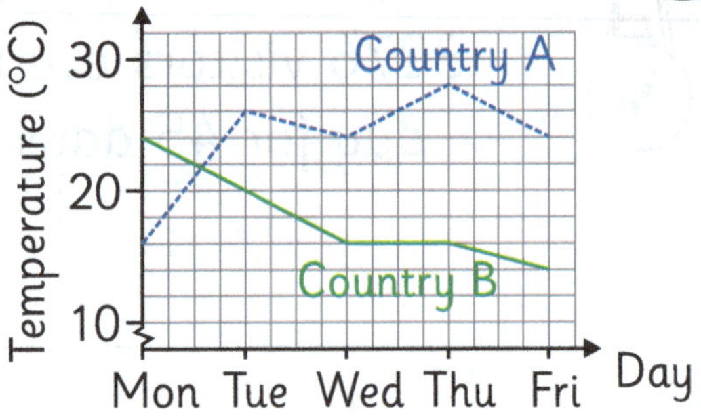

4. ____ °C

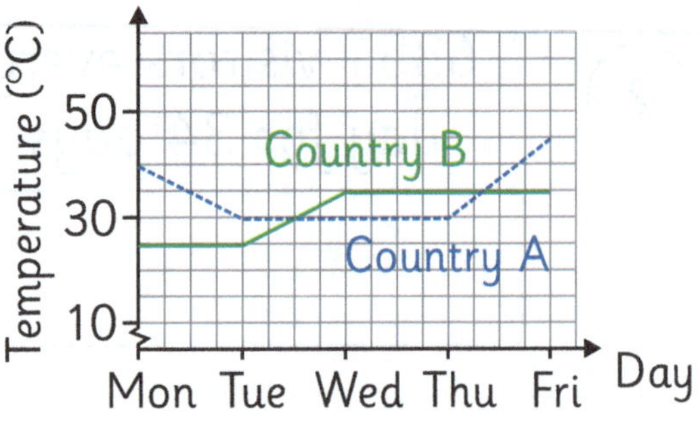

5. ____ °C

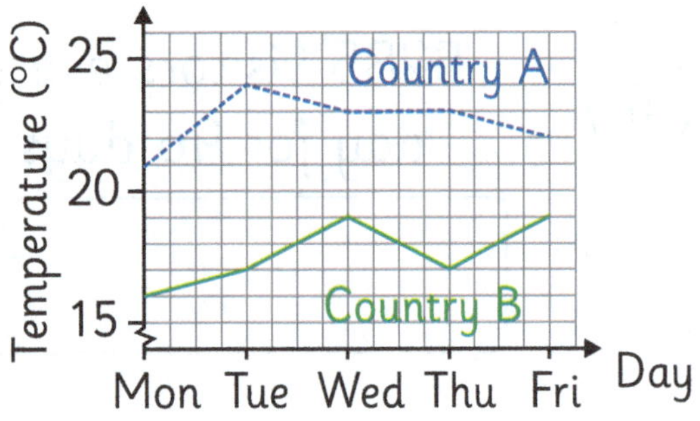

6. 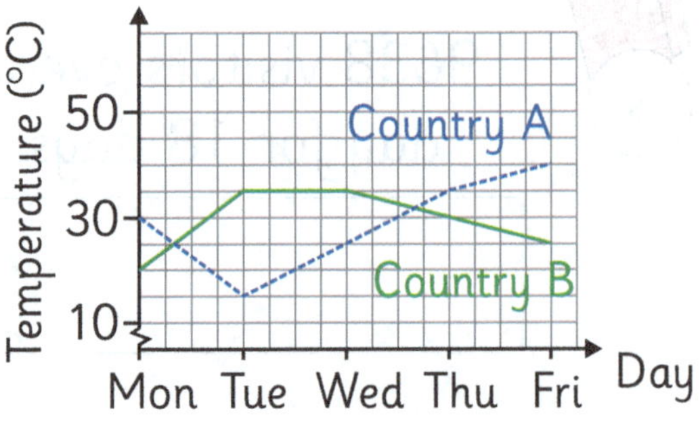 ____ °C

Today I scored ____ out of 6.

Year 6 Maths — Spring Term

Week 1 — Day 5

Is the calculation correct? Tick the answer. $\frac{4}{5} \div 5 = \frac{4}{20}$ Yes ☐ No ☑

1) $\frac{1}{3} \div 2 = \frac{1}{6}$ Yes ☐ No ☐

2) $\frac{2}{7} \div 3 = \frac{2}{21}$ Yes ☐ No ☐

3) $\frac{3}{4} \div 4 = \frac{12}{16}$ Yes ☐ No ☐

4) $\frac{4}{9} \div 4 = \frac{1}{9}$ Yes ☐ No ☐

5) $\frac{6}{9} \div 3 = \frac{1}{3}$ Yes ☐ No ☐

6) $\frac{3}{5} \div 5 = \frac{3}{25}$ Yes ☐ No ☐

7) $\frac{2}{10} \div 3 = \frac{2}{15}$ Yes ☐ No ☐

8) $\frac{3}{6} \div 6 = \frac{1}{6}$ Yes ☐ No ☐

9) $\frac{4}{7} \div 6 = \frac{2}{21}$ Yes ☐ No ☐

10) $\frac{5}{6} \div 5 = \frac{1}{5}$ Yes ☐ No ☐

11) $\frac{3}{12} \div 5 = \frac{1}{20}$ Yes ☐ No ☐

12) $\frac{2}{8} \div 4 = \frac{1}{16}$ Yes ☐ No ☐

Today I scored ☐ out of 12.

Week 2 — Day 1

Use division to write the fraction as a decimal. $\frac{1}{20}$ = 0.05 $20 \overline{)1.^10^{10}0}$ 0.0 5

1) $\frac{1}{8}$ =

2) $\frac{9}{50}$ =

3) $\frac{7}{8}$ =

4) $\frac{7}{20}$ =

5) $\frac{13}{20}$ =

6) $\frac{13}{50}$ =

7) $\frac{19}{20}$ =

8) $\frac{37}{50}$ =

9) $\frac{17}{20}$ =

10) $\frac{33}{50}$ =

11) $\frac{5}{8}$ =

12) $\frac{41}{50}$ =

Today I scored ☐ out of 12.

Week 2 — Day 2

Write the correct answer.   628.2 ÷ 2 = ?   314.1

1) 48.2 ÷ 2 = ?

2) 633.9 ÷ 3 = ?

3) 922.4 ÷ 2 = ?

4) 662.4 ÷ 8 = ?

5) 305.5 ÷ 5 = ?

6) 326.2 ÷ 7 = ?

7) 578.2 ÷ 5 = ?

8) 213.4 ÷ 4 = ?

9) 729.4 ÷ 7 = ?

10) 454.5 ÷ 6 = ?

11) 781.2 ÷ 8 = ?

12) 512.2 ÷ 4 = ?

Today I scored ☐ out of 12.

Week 2 — Day 3

Is the number sentence correct? Tick the right box. $\frac{10}{16} = 5 \div 8$ Yes ✓ No

1. $\frac{15}{20} = 3 \div 4$ Yes / No
2. $\frac{7}{35} = 1 \div 5$ Yes / No
3. $\frac{3}{36} = 1 \div 6$ Yes / No
4. $\frac{18}{63} = 1 \div 4$ Yes / No
5. $\frac{54}{81} = 2 \div 3$ Yes / No
6. $\frac{36}{60} = 3 \div 5$ Yes / No
7. $\frac{14}{36} = 1 \div 4$ Yes / No
8. $\frac{24}{38} = 12 \div 19$ Yes / No
9. $\frac{21}{57} = 7 \div 19$ Yes / No
10. $\frac{36}{72} = 2 \div 3$ Yes / No

Today I scored [ ] out of 10.

Week 2 — Day 4

How much money will the child have left after buying the toys?

Jingyi has £10. She buys 2 teddies. Teddies are £2.50 each.

£5.00

1) Emilia has £20.
She buys 3 basketballs.
Basketballs cost £3.50 each.

£

2) Sebastian has £10.
He buys 7 stickers.
Stickers cost £0.50 each.

£

3) Gareth has £10.
He buys 8 dice.
Dice cost £0.12 each.

£

4) Maitreyi has £30.
She buys 3 toy cars.
Toy cars cost £5.55 each.

£

5) Erin has £20.
She buys 2 robots.
Robots cost £4.36 each.

£

6) Rozalija has £20.
She buys 4 jigsaws.
Jigsaws cost £3.72 each.

£

7) Thea has £10.
She buys 6 frisbees.
Frisbees cost £1.32 each.

£

8) Rachid has £30.
He buys 9 packs of cards.
Packs of cards cost £2.67 each.

£

Today I scored ☐ out of 8.

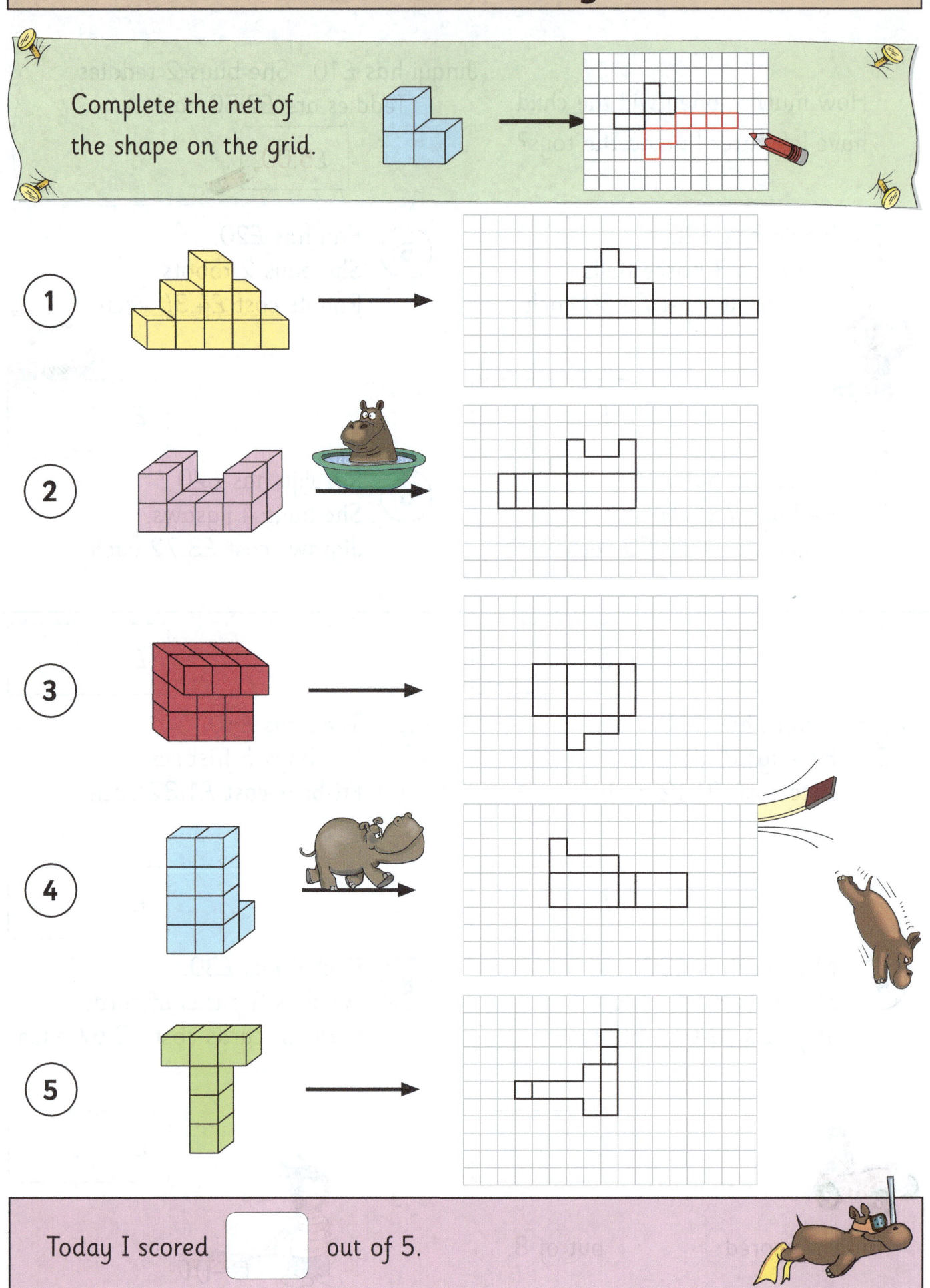

Week 3 — Day 1

Translate the shape.   2 squares up, 4 squares right

① 4 squares down, 6 squares right

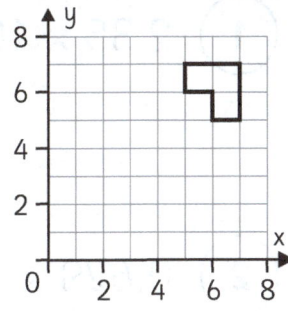

⑤ 5 squares down, 1 square left

② 3 squares down, 5 squares left

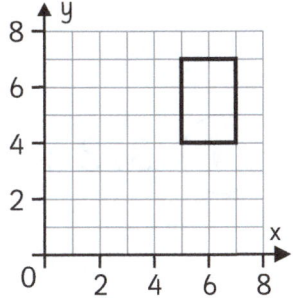

⑥ 2 squares up, 3 squares right

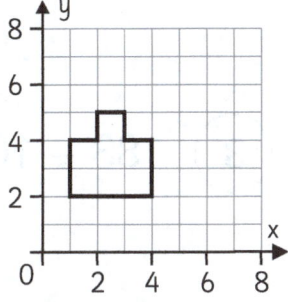

③ 3 squares up, 2 squares right

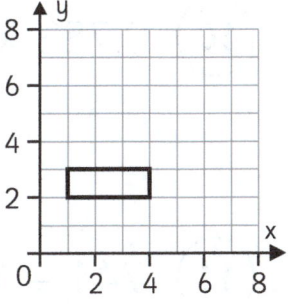

⑦ 1 square down, 3 squares right

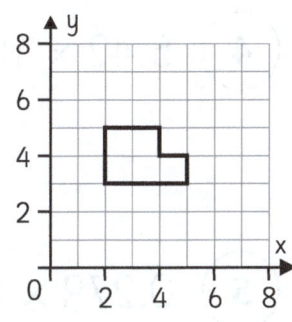

④ 4 squares up, 3 squares left

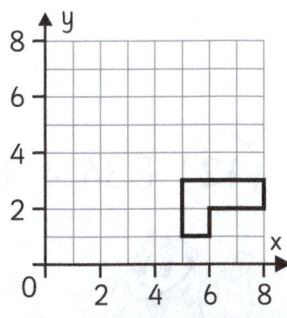

⑧ 3 squares up, 4 squares right

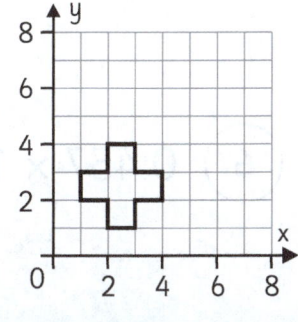

Today I scored  out of 8.

Week 3 — Day 2

Write the answer to the calculation.   5.96 × 100 = 596

1) 2.35 × 100 =

2) 0.629 × 1000 =

3) 183 ÷ 10 =

4) 5.42 × 100 =

5) 0.279 × 10 =

6) 0.457 × 100 =

7) 8.72 ÷ 10 =

8) 9.15 × 1000 =

9) 373 ÷ 1000 =

10) 0.783 × 1000 =

11) 741 ÷ 100 =

12) 834 ÷ 1000 =

Today I scored ☐ out of 12.

Week 3 — Day 3

What percentage of the recipe is not flour? The recipe is $\frac{33}{100}$ flour. 67%

1. The recipe is $\frac{87}{100}$ flour. ___ %

2. The recipe is $\frac{41}{100}$ flour. ___ %

3. The recipe is $\frac{1}{2}$ flour. ___ %

4. The recipe is $\frac{3}{10}$ flour. ___ %

5. The recipe is $\frac{8}{10}$ flour. ___ %

6. The recipe is $\frac{3}{4}$ flour. ___ %

7. The recipe is $\frac{17}{50}$ flour. ___ %

8. The recipe is $\frac{6}{25}$ flour. ___ %

9. The recipe is $\frac{14}{25}$ flour. ___ %

10. The recipe is $\frac{1}{5}$ flour. ___ %

11. The recipe is $\frac{9}{20}$ flour. ___ %

12. The recipe is $\frac{3}{5}$ flour. ___ %

Today I scored ___ out of 12.

Week 3 — Day 4

Write the name of the person who has watched the most of a TV show.

Person	Chloe	Nihal	Jai
Amount watched	$\frac{2}{3}$	$\frac{3}{5}$	65%

Chloe

1

Person	Molly	Levi	Will
Amount watched	70%	$\frac{90}{100}$	$\frac{4}{5}$

5

Person	Stan	Rich	Taryn
Amount watched	$\frac{13}{20}$	$\frac{6}{10}$	55%

2

Person	Adam	Jade	Kate
Amount watched	41%	$\frac{1}{4}$	$\frac{37}{100}$

6

Person	Abe	Mary	Rafe
Amount watched	$\frac{7}{20}$	$\frac{1}{3}$	37%

3

Person	Otto	Cali	Dean
Amount watched	$\frac{4}{5}$	$\frac{17}{20}$	82%

7

Person	Bert	Priti	Flo
Amount watched	73%	$\frac{19}{25}$	$\frac{3}{4}$

4

Person	Hazel	Finn	Lana
Amount watched	$\frac{2}{5}$	46%	$\frac{1}{2}$

8

Person	Lee	Suki	Rose
Amount watched	$\frac{4}{25}$	14%	$\frac{3}{20}$

Today I scored ☐ out of 8.

Week 3 — Day 5

Who has run further?

Ben has run 30% of 200 m
Jon has run 20% of 400 m

[Jon] has run further.

1. Leo has run 50% of 100 m
   Amy has run 30% of 300 m
   [ ] has run further.

2. Raj has run 40% of 500 m
   Mike has run 80% of 200 m
   [ ] has run further.

3. Ella has run 25% of 200 m
   Hina has run 60% of 100 m
   [ ] has run further.

4. Kubo has run 60% of 900 m
   Liam has run 85% of 700 m
   [ ] has run further.

5. Liz has run 65% of 400 m
   Dora has run 81% of 300 m
   [ ] has run further.

6. Jim has run 12% of 800 m
   Sofi has run 15% of 600 m
   [ ] has run further.

7. Sam has run 52% of 700 m
   Kyle has run 86% of 500 m
   [ ] has run further.

8. Mia has run 38% of 300 m
   Juan has run 23% of 400 m
   [ ] has run further.

Today I scored [ ] out of 8.

Week 4 — Day 1

Circle the number that is not a common factor of the two numbers.

18 and 30
2   6   3   **(9)**

1. 16 and 24
2   3   8   4

2. 64 and 80
5   2   8

3. 63 and 81
9   7   3

4. 20 and 32
4   2   1   8

5. 24 and 16
2   8   6   4

6. 48 and 80
8   16   12

7. 36 and 54
12   9   6

8. 36 and 42
3   6   2   9

9. 56 and 28
7   8   2   4

10. 72 and 48
6   3   8   16

11. 48 and 60
12   6   3   8

12. 96 and 84
12   4   7   3

Today I scored ☐ out of 12.

Week 4 — Day 2

How many lines of symmetry and acute angles does the shape have?

regular octagon

lines of symmetry	8
acute angles	0

1. square

lines of symmetry	
acute angles	

2. rectangle

lines of symmetry	
acute angles	

3. equilateral triangle

lines of symmetry	
acute angles	

4. parallelogram

lines of symmetry	
acute angles	

5. regular pentagon

lines of symmetry	
acute angles	

6. rhombus

lines of symmetry	
acute angles	

7. regular hexagon

lines of symmetry	
acute angles	

8. heptagon

lines of symmetry	
acute angles	

Today I scored ☐ out of 8.

Week 4 — Day 3

Circle the number that correctly starts the sentence.

165 000   (161 000)   154 000

? rounded to the nearest 10 000 is 160 000.

1) 620 000   760 000   690 000

? rounded to the nearest 100 000 is 700 000.

2) 561 000   567 000   572 000

? rounded to the nearest 10 000 is 560 000.

3) 9 448 200   9 436 200   9 445 800

? rounded to the nearest 10 000 is 9 440 000.

4) 8 139 070   8 165 220   8 045 310

? rounded to the nearest 100 000 is 8 100 000.

5) 2 453 650   2 453 101   2 452 402

? rounded to the nearest 1000 is 2 453 000.

6) 5 873 893   5 878 562   5 885 385

? rounded to the nearest 10 000 is 5 880 000.

Today I scored ☐ out of 6.

Week 4 — Day 4

Complete the sentence. £550 is split between Robert and David. For every £4 Robert gets, David gets £1. David gets £110.

1) £260 is split between Mel and Sue. For every £3 Mel gets, Sue gets £1.

Sue gets £ _____ .

2) £180 is split between Paul and Barry. For every £1 Paul gets, Barry gets £2.

Barry gets £ _____ .

3) £720 is split between Stephen and Hugh. For every £5 Stephen gets, Hugh gets £1.

Hugh gets £ _____ .

4) £450 is split between Jennifer and Dawn. For every £3 Jennifer gets, Dawn gets £2.

Dawn gets £ _____ .

5) £630 is split between Meera and Sanjeev. For every £2 Meera gets, Sanjeev gets £5.

Sanjeev gets £ _____ .

6) £480 is split between Victoria and Julie. For every £3 Victoria gets, Julie gets £5.

Julie gets £ _____ .

7) £840 is split between Stan and Oliver. For every £4 Stan gets, Oliver gets £3.

Oliver gets £ _____ .

8) £540 is split between Thelma and Louise. For every £7 Thelma gets, Louise gets £2.

Louise gets £ _____ .

Today I scored _____ out of 8.

Week 4 — Day 5

Plant pots are split into two groups. How many pots are in the smaller group?

45 pots split in the ratio 2 : 3

18 pots

1. 60 pots split in the ratio 4 : 1 — ___ pots
2. 32 pots split in the ratio 3 : 1 — ___ pots
3. 36 pots split in the ratio 1 : 5 — ___ pots
4. 25 pots split in the ratio 2 : 3 — ___ pots
5. 49 pots split in the ratio 5 : 2 — ___ pots
6. 54 pots split in the ratio 5 : 4 — ___ pots
7. 77 pots split in the ratio 6 : 5 — ___ pots
8. 48 pots split in the ratio 7 : 5 — ___ pots
9. 63 pots split in the ratio 2 : 7 — ___ pots
10. 121 pots split in the ratio 7 : 4 — ___ pots
11. 96 pots split in the ratio 3 : 5 — ___ pots
12. 108 pots split in the ratio 5 : 7 — ___ pots

Today I scored ___ out of 12.

Year 6 Maths — Spring Term

Week 5 — Day 1

At a farm, 1 in every 3 pigs has spots. Complete the sentence.

There are 12 pigs in total. **4 pigs** have spots.

1. There are 9 pigs in total. ___ pigs have spots.

2. There are 18 pigs in total. ___ pigs have spots.

3. There are 15 pigs in total. ___ pigs have spots.

4. There are ___ pigs in total. 10 pigs have spots.

5. There are ___ pigs in total. 12 pigs have spots.

6. There are 27 pigs in total. ___ pigs have spots.

7. There are ___ pigs in total. 20 pigs have spots.

8. There are 69 pigs in total. ___ pigs have spots.

9. There are 300 pigs in total. ___ pigs have spots.

10. There are 210 pigs in total. ___ pigs have spots.

11. There are ___ pigs in total. 200 pigs have spots.

12. There are ___ pigs in total. 150 pigs have spots.

Today I scored ___ out of 12.

Week 5 — Day 2

The shape is enlarged by the scale factor shown. What is the total height of the enlarged shape?

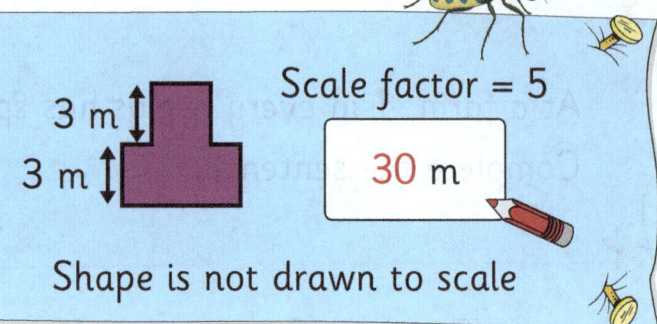

Shape is not drawn to scale

1 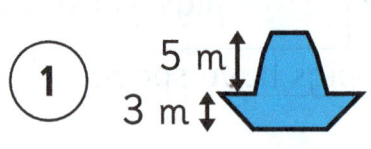 Scale factor = 3 ☐ m

6 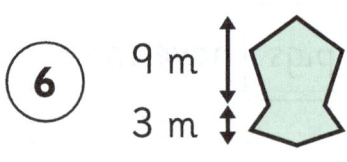 Scale factor = 6 ☐ m

2 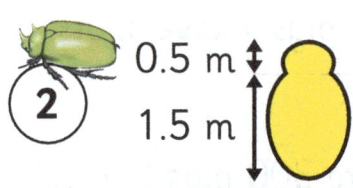 Scale factor = 11 ☐ m

7 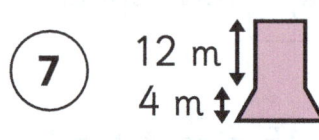 Scale factor = 3 ☐ m

3 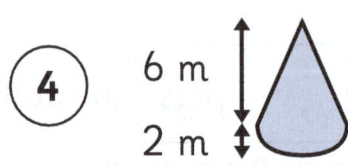 Scale factor = 7 ☐ m

8 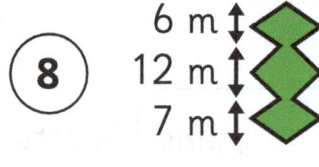 Scale factor = 8 ☐ m

4 Scale factor = 4 ☐ m

9 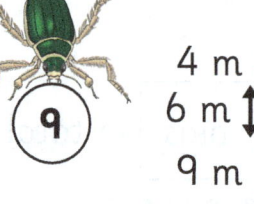 Scale factor = 3 ☐ m

5 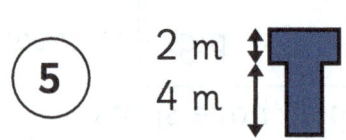 Scale factor = 5 ☐ m

10 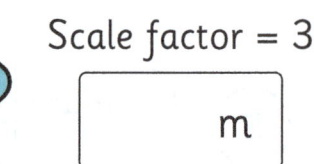 Scale factor = 7 ☐ m

Today I scored ☐ out of 10.

Week 5 — Day 3

For every 2 pizzas Giovanna sells, she sells 7 bowls of spaghetti. Complete the sentence.

Giovanna sells 4 pizzas and 14 bowls of spaghetti.

1) Giovanna sells 6 pizzas and ☐ bowls of spaghetti.

2) Giovanna sells ☐ pizzas and 28 bowls of spaghetti.

3) Giovanna sells 10 pizzas and ☐ bowls of spaghetti.

4) Giovanna sells 12 pizzas and ☐ bowls of spaghetti.

5) Giovanna sells ☐ pizzas and 70 bowls of spaghetti.

6) Giovanna sells 22 pizzas and ☐ bowls of spaghetti.

7) Giovanna sells ☐ pizzas and 140 bowls of spaghetti.

8) Giovanna sells 30 pizzas and ☐ bowls of spaghetti.

9) Giovanna sells 140 pizzas and ☐ bowls of spaghetti.

10) Giovanna sells ☐ pizzas and 175 bowls of spaghetti.

Today I scored ☐ out of 10.

Week 5 — Day 4

The widths of the shapes are shown. What is the scale factor of enlargement from the smaller shape to the bigger shape?

5 cm   0.3 m   6

Shapes are not drawn to scale

1. 12 cm   0.36 m

2. 8 cm   0.4 m

3. 6 cm   0.24 m

4. 12 cm   1.44 m

5. 40 cm   1.2 m

6. 30 cm   2.7 m

7. 25 cm   1.5 m

8. 0.8 cm   0.08 m

Today I scored ☐ out of 8.

Week 5 — Day 5

Each box contains the same number of buttons. Talia counts the total number of buttons. Has she counted the buttons correctly? Tick the correct box.

There are 8 boxes. Talia counts 1616 buttons.

Yes ✓   No ☐

1 There are 17 boxes. Talia counts 3757 buttons.

Yes ☐   No ☐

2 There are 11 boxes. Talia counts 2845 buttons.

Yes ☐   No ☐

3 There are 16 boxes. Talia counts 6720 buttons.

Yes ☐   No ☐

4 There are 13 boxes. Talia counts 5616 buttons.

Yes ☐   No ☐

5 There are 33 boxes. Talia counts 6963 buttons.

Yes ☐   No ☐

6 There are 12 boxes. Talia counts 2222 buttons.

Yes ☐   No ☐

7 There are 14 boxes. Talia counts 4432 buttons.

Yes ☐   No ☐

8 There are 21 boxes. Talia counts 8946 buttons.

Yes ☐   No ☐

Today I scored ☐ out of 8.

Week 6 — Day 1

Write the rule for the sequence. 4 10 16 22   add 6

1) 8 13 18 23

2) 4 11 18 25

3) 35 31 27 23

4) 62 71 80 89

5) 460 430 400 370

6) 31 19 7 −5

7) −28 −15 −2 11

8) 11 5 −1 −7

9) 6 −14 −34 −54

10) −10 25 60 95

11) −5 −22 −39 −56

12) −49 −31 −13 5

Today I scored ☐ out of 12.

Week 6 — Day 2

Write <, > or = to show how the two values being described compare to each other.

721 632 rounded to the nearest 1000. = 722 480 rounded to the nearest 1000.

1) 145 200 rounded to the nearest 1000. ☐ 145 770 rounded to the nearest 1000.

2) 457 208 rounded to the nearest 10 000. ☐ 461 315 rounded to the nearest 1000.

3) 5 846 009 rounded to the nearest 10 000. ☐ 5 853 966 rounded to the nearest 10 000.

4) 8 216 491 rounded to the nearest 1000. ☐ 8 215 920 rounded to the nearest 100.

5) 6 414 067 rounded to the nearest 1000. ☐ 6 415 873 rounded to the nearest 100.

6) 3 564 641 rounded to the nearest 1000. ☐ 3 560 048 rounded to the nearest 10 000.

7) 2 111 999 rounded to the nearest 10 000. ☐ 2 109 991 rounded to the nearest 1000.

Today I scored ☐ out of 7.

Week 6 — Day 3

The formula for the term in position n of a sequence is given. Write the first 3 terms of the sequence.

3n + 2

| 5 | 8 | 11 |

1) 2n + 8

2) 5n + 4

3) 4n − 3

4) 8n + 7

5) 6n − 4

6) 9n + 11

7) 12n − 9

8) 4n − 6

9) 7n − 16

10) 5n − 12

11) 12n − 17

12) 8n − 18

Today I scored ☐ out of 12.

Week 6 — Day 4

Use the formula to work out the total cost of buying the furniture and having it delivered.

Total cost = £15 × Number of chairs + £20

Total cost of 6 chairs = £110

1) Total cost = £60 × Number of tables + £40

   Total cost of 3 tables = £

2) Total cost = £120 × Number of sofas + £30

   Total cost of 2 sofas = £

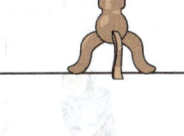

3) Total cost = £68 × Number of wardrobes + £15

   Total cost of 5 wardrobes = £

4) Total cost = £265 × Number of beds + £110

   Total cost of 3 beds = £

5) Total cost = £80.50 × Number of armchairs + £18

   Total cost of 8 armchairs = £

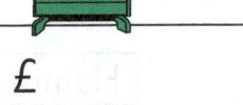

6) Total cost = £24.50 × Number of bookshelves + £27

   Total cost of 7 bookshelves = £

Today I scored ☐ out of 6.

Week 6 — Day 5

Who had the shortest appointment?

	Appointment	
	Start time	End time
Richard	14:10	15:16
Fiona	10:15	11:17
Patrick	07:50	09:01

1)

	Appointment	
	Start time	End time
Carrie	08:00	10:21
Jack	09:20	11:06
Nikhil	12:40	15:44

4)

	Appointment	
	Start time	End time
Ming	16:05	18:37
Hitesh	18:55	21:31
Alice	15:30	18:08

2)

	Appointment	
	Start time	End time
Leena	12:45	13:57
Holly	15:10	16:23
Joyce	09:05	10:09

5)

	Appointment	
	Start time	End time
Katie	11:15	14:57
Albert	13:45	17:24
Steph	09:50	13:32

3)

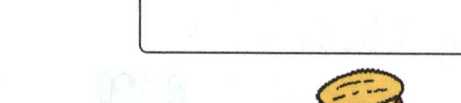

	Appointment	
	Start time	End time
Hamish	06:50	08:12
Ulrich	10:25	11:49
John	08:10	09:21

6)

	Appointment	
	Start time	End time
Ines	15:40	20:34
Farhad	12:55	17:47
Louis	17:05	21:58

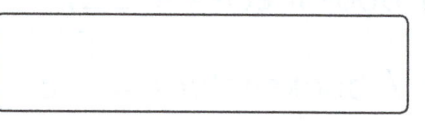

Today I scored ☐ out of 6.

Week 7 — Day 1

Rearrange the digits to make the number described.

6 451 826
The largest even number
8 665 412

1) 1 037 285
The largest even number

2) 5 298 746
The smallest even number

3) 4 782 583
The largest odd number

4) 8 364 554
The largest even number

5) 2 142 859
The smallest even number

6) 3 314 842
The smallest odd number

7) 4 388 646
The smallest odd number

8) 7 824 908
The largest odd number

Today I scored ☐ out of 8.

Week 7 — Day 2

The shapes in the equation stand for whole numbers bigger than 0. List all the possible pairs of values of the shapes.

$4 \times \square + \bigcirc = 11$

$\square = 1 \quad \bigcirc = 7$

$\square = 2 \quad \bigcirc = 3$

1) $6 \times \square + \bigcirc = 14$

$\square = \quad \bigcirc =$

$\square = \quad \bigcirc =$

2) $3 \times \square + \bigcirc = 10$

$\square = \quad \bigcirc =$

$\square = \quad \bigcirc =$

$\square = \quad \bigcirc =$

3) $7 \times \square + \bigcirc = 23$

$\square = \quad \bigcirc =$

$\square = \quad \bigcirc =$

$\square = \quad \bigcirc =$

4) $8 \times \square + \bigcirc = 18$

$\square = \quad \bigcirc =$

$\square = \quad \bigcirc =$

5) $10 \div \square + \bigcirc = 8$

$\square = \quad \bigcirc =$

$\square = \quad \bigcirc =$

$\square = \quad \bigcirc =$

6) $21 \div \square - \bigcirc = 2$

$\square = \quad \bigcirc =$

$\square = \quad \bigcirc =$

$\square = \quad \bigcirc =$

Today I scored ☐ out of 6.

Year 6 Maths — Spring Term

Week 7 — Day 3

A bag contains 120 marbles. How many of the marbles are both blue and plastic?

$\frac{2}{3}$ of the marbles are blue and $\frac{3}{4}$ of the blue marbles are plastic.

60 marbles

1) $\frac{1}{6}$ of the marbles are blue and $\frac{1}{2}$ of the blue marbles are plastic.

☐ marbles

2) $\frac{5}{6}$ of the marbles are blue and $\frac{4}{5}$ of the blue marbles are plastic.

☐ marbles

3) $\frac{1}{3}$ of the marbles are blue and $\frac{9}{10}$ of the blue marbles are plastic.

☐ marbles

4) $\frac{1}{2}$ of the marbles are blue and $\frac{5}{12}$ of the blue marbles are plastic.

☐ marbles

5) $\frac{11}{12}$ of the marbles are blue and $\frac{1}{5}$ of the blue marbles are plastic.

☐ marbles

6) $\frac{7}{10}$ of the marbles are blue and $\frac{1}{4}$ of the blue marbles are plastic.

☐ marbles

7) $\frac{3}{5}$ of the marbles are blue and $\frac{1}{3}$ of the blue marbles are plastic.

☐ marbles

8) $\frac{3}{8}$ of the marbles are blue and $\frac{4}{9}$ of the blue marbles are plastic.

☐ marbles

Today I scored ☐ out of 8.

Week 7 — Day 4

From the information given, write an equation involving x and give the value of x.

If you multiply x by 7 and add 2 you get 23.

7x + 2 = 23 and x = 3

1 If you multiply x by 3 you get 15.

☐ and x = ☐

2 If you multiply x by 8 you get 24.

☐ and x = ☐

3 If you multiply x by 7 you get 49.

☐ and x = ☐

4 If you multiply x by 6 and subtract 6 you get 18.

☐ and x = ☐

5 If you multiply x by 2 and subtract 3 you get 13.

☐ and x = ☐

6 If you multiply x by 9 and add 7 you get 34.

☐ and x = ☐

7 If you multiply x by 4 and add 9 you get 45.

☐ and x = ☐

8 If you multiply x by 8 and subtract 5 you get 51.

☐ and x = ☐

Today I scored ☐ out of 8.

Week 7 — Day 5

Circle the pair of values for which both of the equations are true.

$A + B = 7$
$4A + B = 13$

A = 3, B = 1   A = 3, B = 4   **(A = 2, B = 5)**

1. $A - B = 6$; $2A + B = 15$

A = 7, B = 1   A = 4, B = 7   A = 9, B = 3

2. $A + B = 8$; $3A - B = 12$

A = 6, B = 2   A = 7, B = 9   A = 5, B = 3

3. $A + B = 12$; $5A + B = 24$

A = 4, B = 8   A = 3, B = 9   A = 7, B = 5

4. $A - B = 2$; $3A + 2B = 26$

A = 7, B = 5   A = 4, B = 7   A = 6, B = 4

5. $A + 2B = 12$; $4A + B = 34$

A = 6, B = 3   A = 8, B = 2   A = 7, B = 6

6. $6A - B = 1$; $4A + 2B = 14$

A = 1, B = 5   A = 2, B = 11   A = 2, B = 3

7. $2A + B = 22$; $2A + 3B = 34$

A = 8, B = 6   A = 9, B = 4   A = 2, B = 10

8. $3A - B = 21$; $2A + 2B = 30$

A = 8, B = 3   A = 10, B = 5   A = 9, B = 6

Today I scored ☐ out of 8.

Week 8 — Day 1

Work out the multiplication.   3.52 × 5 = 17.6

1) 1.25 × 3 =

2) 4.56 × 6 =

3) 3.47 × 4 =

4) 5.08 × 7 =

5) 4.46 × 8 =

6) 6.97 × 9 =

7) 3.43 × 9 =

8) 2.73 × 6 =

9) 8.62 × 7 =

10) 9.99 × 9 =

11) 7.72 × 6 =

12) 9.63 × 8 =

Today I scored ☐ out of 12.

Week 8 — Day 2

Use a ruler and protractor to draw the parallelogram.

Sides: 2 cm and 3 cm
Angles: 40° and 140°

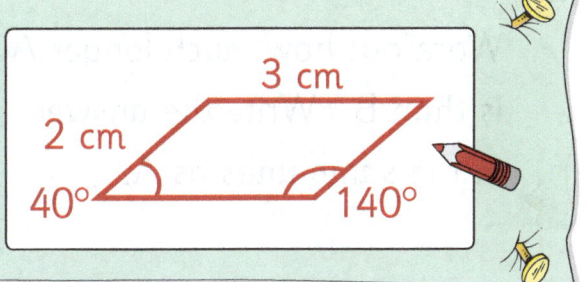

1. Sides: 1 cm and 4 cm
   Angles: 30° and 150°

2. Sides: 3 cm and 3 cm
   Angles: 60° and 120°

3. Sides: 3 cm and 4 cm
   Angles: 75° and 105°

4. Sides: 2 cm and 4.5 cm
   Angles: 85° and 95°

5. Sides: 3.4 cm and 4.2 cm
   Angles: 55° and 125°

Today I scored ☐ out of 5.

Week 8 — Day 3

Work out how much longer A is than B. Write the answer in the same units as A.

A = 3.746 cm
B = 22.41 mm

1.505 cm

1) A = 6846 m
B = 6.022 km
_____ m

2) A = 160.4 cm
B = 1.301 m
_____ cm

3) A = 8928 mm
B = 809.7 cm
_____ mm

4) A = 779.3 cm
B = 6.587 m
_____ cm

5) A = 5.629 cm
B = 33.92 mm
_____ cm

6) A = 2.873 km
B = 2536 m
_____ km

7) A = 8.329 cm
B = 58.37 mm
_____ cm

8) A = 36 007 m
B = 35.212 km
_____ m

9) A = 7.834 m
B = 686.3 cm
_____ m

10) A = 4.329 km
B = 2588 m
_____ km

Today I scored ____ out of 10.

Week 8 — Day 4

8 km is approximately equal to 5 miles. Rani and Toby measure how far they run each month. Convert Rani's distance into miles and then tick the box next to the person who runs further.

Rani = 8 km ☐
Toby = 6 miles ✓

1) Rani = 16 km ☐
   Toby = 9 miles ☐

2) Rani = 48 km ☐
   Toby = 32 miles ☐

3) Rani = 40 km ☐
   Toby = 22 miles ☐

4) Rani = 88 km ☐
   Toby = 57 miles ☐

5) Rani = 72 km ☐
   Toby = 43 miles ☐

6) Rani = 80 km ☐
   Toby = 48 miles ☐

7) Rani = 56 km ☐
   Toby = 37 miles ☐

8) Rani = 320 km ☐
   Toby = 197 miles ☐

9) Rani = 240 km ☐
   Toby = 163 miles ☐

10) Rani = 120 km ☐
    Toby = 78 miles ☐

Today I scored ☐ out of 10.

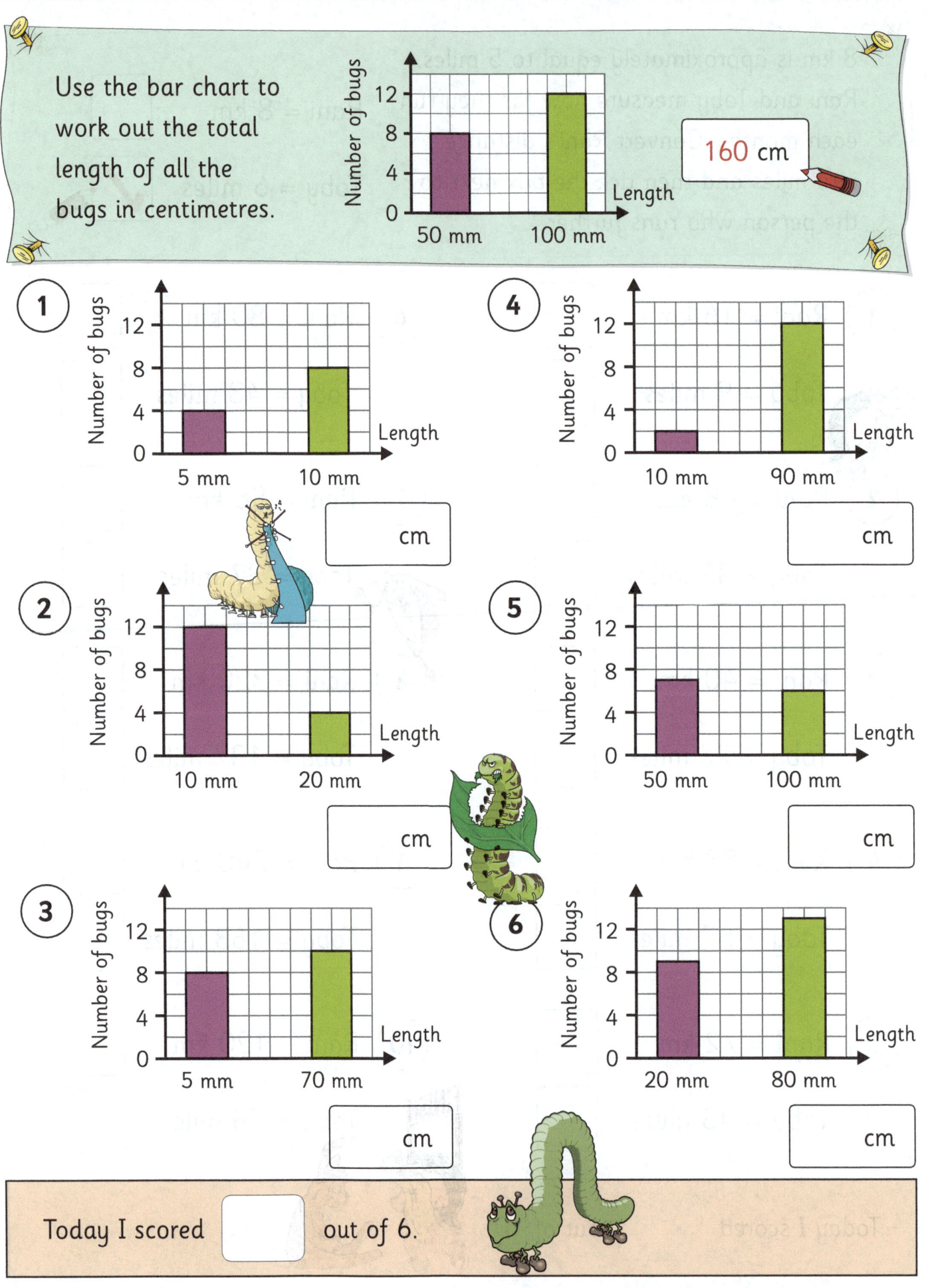

Week 9 — Day 1

Circle the two equivalent fractions.

$1\frac{2}{5}$ ⓐ$\frac{36}{15}$ ⓐ$\frac{12}{5}$ $\frac{24}{15}$

1. $\frac{9}{6}$ $\frac{4}{3}$ $\frac{7}{6}$ $\frac{3}{2}$

2. $\frac{4}{5}$ $\frac{8}{10}$ $\frac{3}{5}$ $\frac{15}{20}$

3. $\frac{16}{12}$ $\frac{12}{16}$ $\frac{7}{8}$ $\frac{3}{4}$

4. $\frac{50}{48}$ $\frac{15}{6}$ $\frac{13}{12}$ $\frac{26}{24}$

5. $2\frac{3}{8}$ $\frac{11}{4}$ $\frac{33}{16}$ $\frac{22}{8}$

6. $\frac{27}{5}$ $5\frac{4}{5}$ $\frac{58}{10}$ $5\frac{10}{15}$

7. $4\frac{3}{16}$ $\frac{11}{2}$ $4\frac{1}{2}$ $\frac{36}{8}$

8. $2\frac{2}{5}$ $2\frac{5}{15}$ $\frac{22}{10}$ $2\frac{4}{10}$

9. $\frac{9}{6}$ $\frac{12}{8}$ $\frac{12}{5}$ $2\frac{2}{8}$

10. $\frac{7}{2}$ $\frac{18}{5}$ $3\frac{5}{10}$ $3\frac{4}{5}$

Today I scored ☐ out of 10.

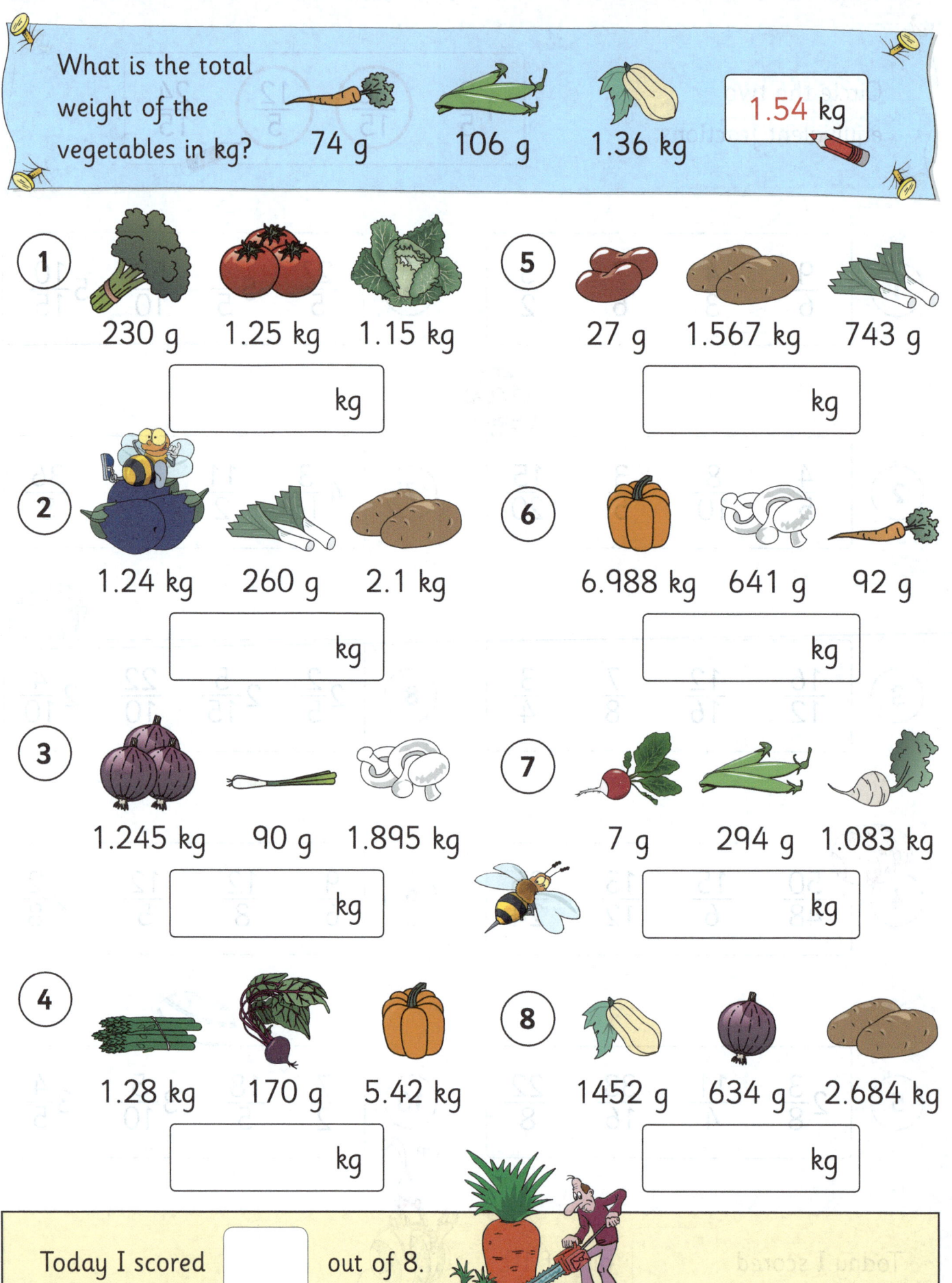

Week 9 — Day 3

Convert the time into seconds.   2 hours and 15 minutes = 8100 seconds

1) 33 minutes = ____ seconds

2) 27 minutes = ____ seconds

3) 51 minutes = ____ seconds

4) 24 minutes = ____ seconds

5) 3 hours = ____ seconds

6) 9 hours = ____ seconds

7) 16 hours = ____ seconds

8) 8 hours and 20 minutes = ____ seconds

9) 4 hours and 10 minutes = ____ seconds

10) 5 hours and 30 minutes = ____ seconds

Today I scored ____ out of 10.

Week 9 — Day 4

How many millilitres of oil are left in the bottle once the amounts shown have been poured out?

2 litres — 340 ml — 1.04 l — **620** ml

1. 3 litres — 580 ml — 1.32 l — ___ ml
2. 5 litres — 350 ml — 2.45 l — ___ ml
3. 4 litres — 640 ml — 2.25 l — ___ ml
4. 6 litres — 270 ml — 5.21 l — ___ ml
5. 8 litres — 555 ml — 6.63 l — ___ ml
6. 6 litres — 735 ml — 2.56 l — ___ ml
7. 9.5 litres — 340 ml — 1.94 l — ___ ml
8. 8.5 litres — 940 ml — 5.87 l — ___ ml

Today I scored ___ out of 8.

Year 6 Maths — Spring Term

Week 9 — Day 5

Correctly complete the sentence.

A machine makes 18 ornaments every day. In 22 weeks, the machine makes 2772 ornaments.

1. A machine makes 40 ornaments every day. In 20 weeks, the machine makes _____ ornaments.

2. A machine makes 24 ornaments every day. In 10 weeks, the machine makes _____ ornaments.

3. A machine makes 30 ornaments every day. In 14 weeks, the machine makes _____ ornaments.

4. A machine makes 15 ornaments every day. In 12 weeks, the machine makes _____ ornaments.

5. A machine makes 35 ornaments every day. In 17 weeks, the machine makes _____ ornaments.

6. A machine makes 52 ornaments every day. In 23 weeks, the machine makes _____ ornaments.

7. A machine makes 84 ornaments every day. In 43 weeks, the machine makes _____ ornaments.

8. A machine makes 97 ornaments every day. In 56 weeks, the machine makes _____ ornaments.

Today I scored _____ out of 8.

Week 10 — Day 1

Work out the size of angles x and y.

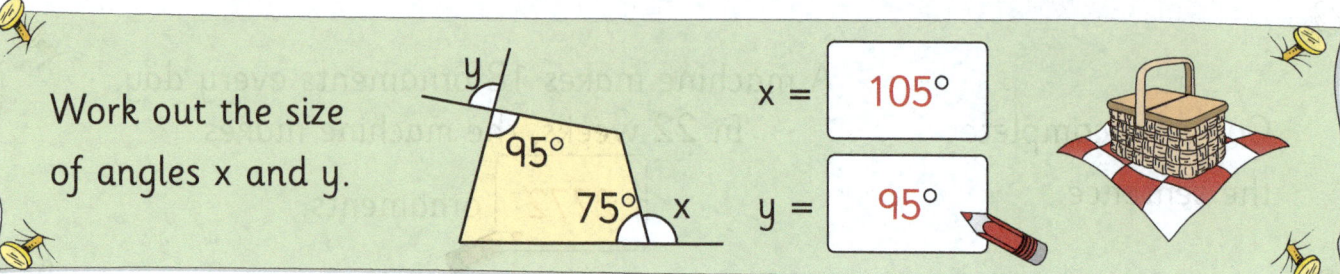

x = 105°
y = 95°

1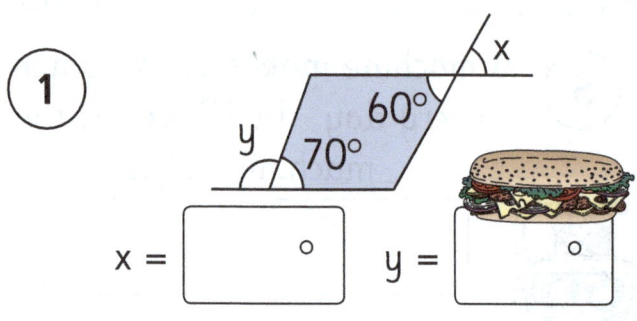

x =   °   y =   °

5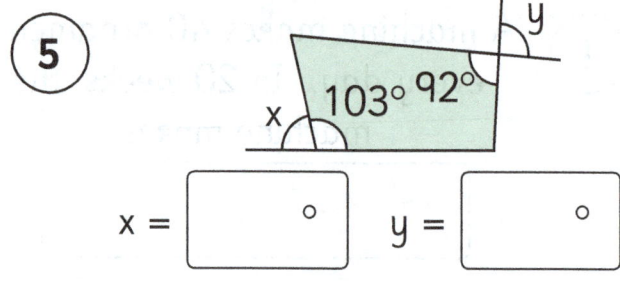

x =   °   y =   °

2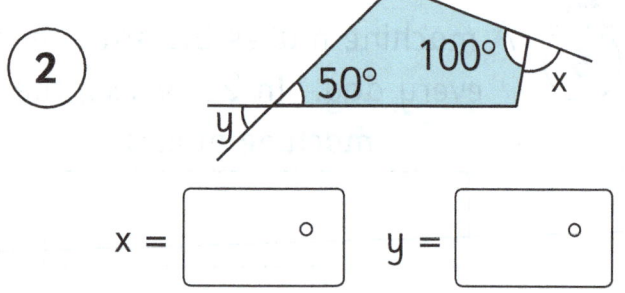

x =   °   y =   °

6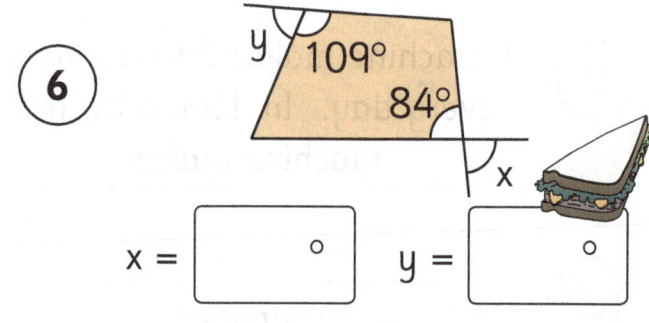

x =   °   y =   °

3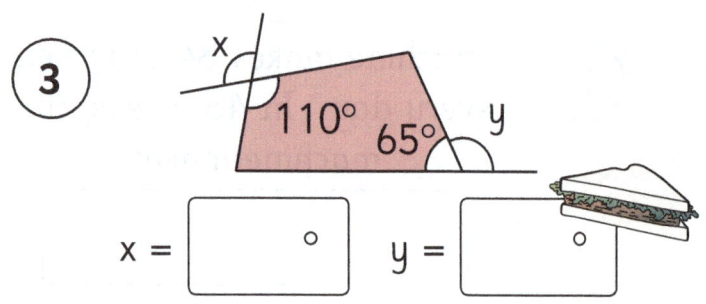

x =   °   y =   °

7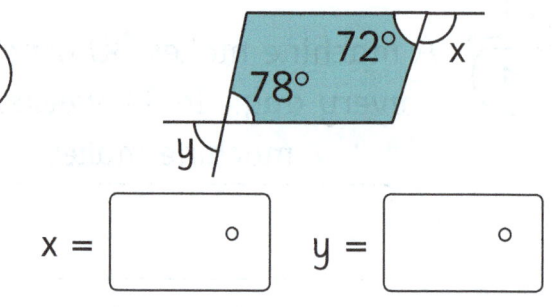

x =   °   y =   °

4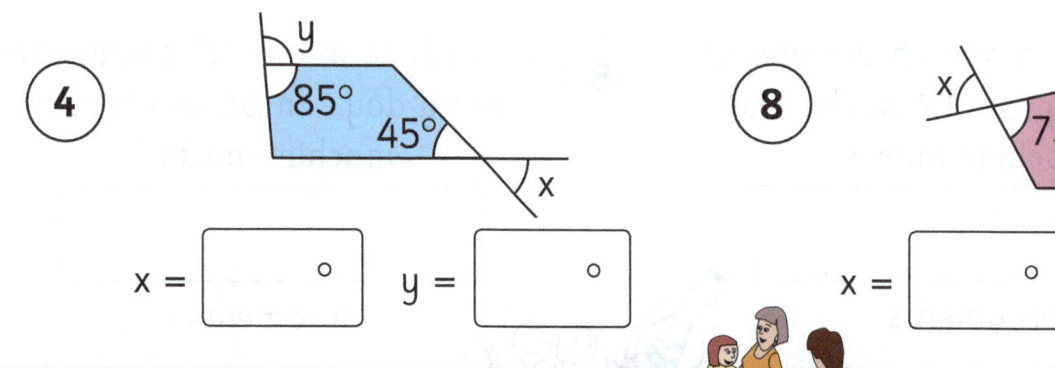

x =   °   y =   °

8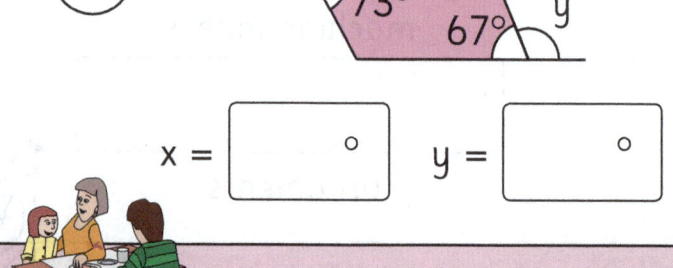

x =   °   y =   °

Today I scored   out of 8.

Week 10 — Day 2

Work out the value of the angle labelled a.

55°

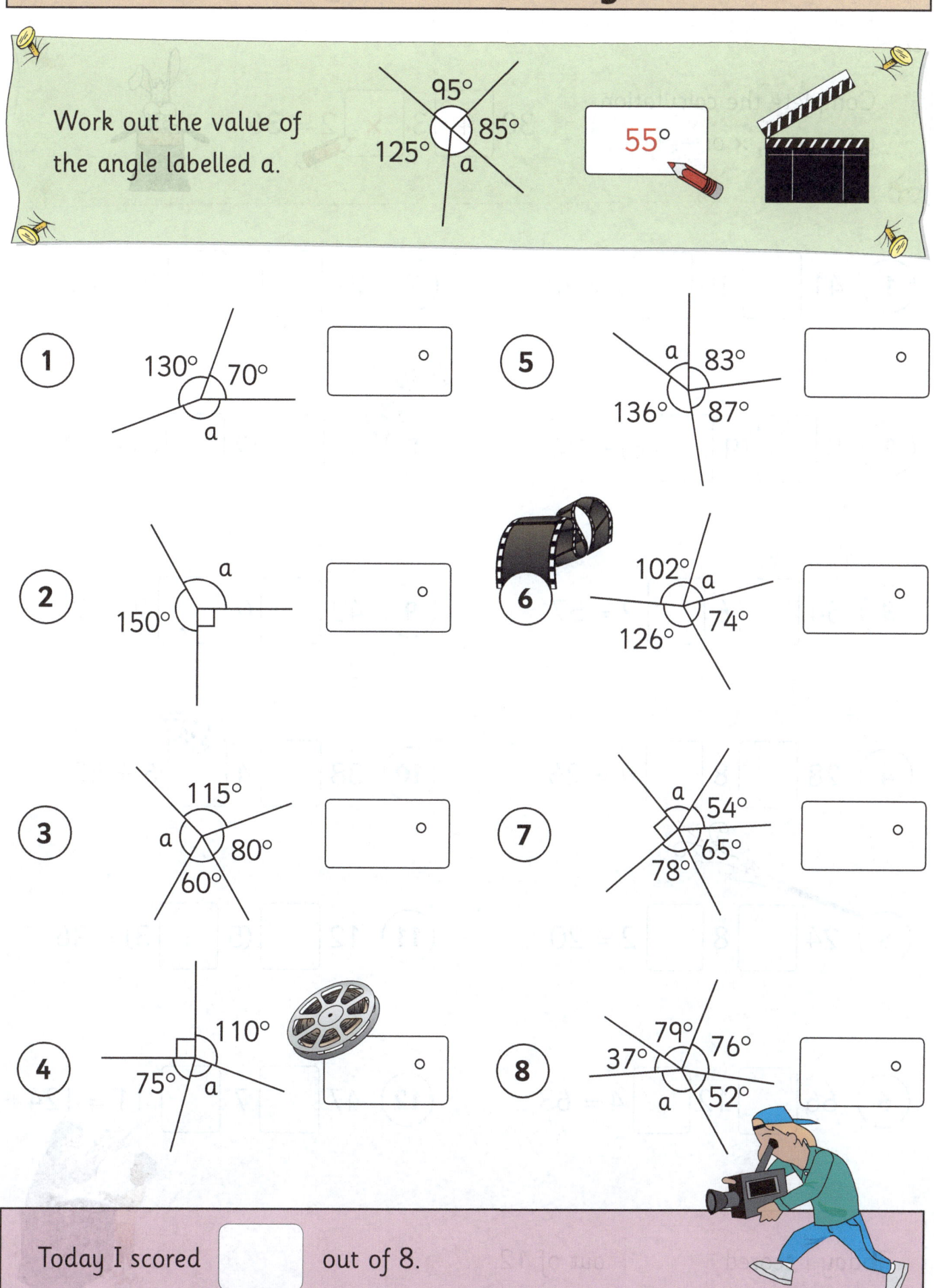

1) 160°

2) 120°

3) 105°

4) 85°

5) 54°

6) 58°

7) 73°

8) 116°

Today I scored ☐ out of 8.

Week 10 — Day 3

Complete the calculation using +, −, × or ÷.   30 [+] 3 [×] 2 = 36

1) 41 [ ] 10 [ ] 2 = 46

2) 8 [ ] (9 [ ] 6) = 24

3) 54 [ ] 6 [ ] 2 = 57

4) 28 [ ] 8 [ ] 4 = 26

5) 24 [ ] 8 [ ] 2 = 20

6) 66 [ ] 12 [ ] 4 = 63

7) 27 [ ] 4 [ ] 3 = 15

8) 36 [ ] (7 [ ] 4) = 12

9) 42 [ ] (4 [ ] 2) = 7

10) 38 [ ] 4 [ ] 6 = 62

11) 12 [ ] (5 [ ] 3) = 96

12) 47 [ ] 7 [ ] 11 = 124

Today I scored [ ] out of 12.

Week 10 — Day 4

Complete the sentence. A quadrilateral has angles of 105°, 60°, 85° and **110°**.

1) A triangle has angles of 20°, 70° and ☐°.

2) A triangle has angles of 80°, 35° and ☐°.

3) A quadrilateral has angles of 100°, 45°, 95° and ☐°.

4) A triangle has angles of 55°, 75° and ☐°.

5) A quadrilateral has angles of 80°, 60°, 85° and ☐°.

6) A quadrilateral has angles of 94°, 76°, 120° and ☐°.

7) A triangle has angles of 73°, 47° and ☐°.

8) A quadrilateral has angles of 96°, 103°, 81° and ☐°.

9) A triangle has angles of 57°, 88° and ☐°.

10) A quadrilateral has angles of 102°, 64°, 93° and ☐°.

Today I scored ☐ out of 10.

Week 10 — Day 5

The exterior angles of a polygon add up to 360°. Write down the sizes of the exterior and interior angles of the polygon.

A 3-sided regular polygon
exterior: 120° interior: 60°

1 A 4-sided regular polygon
exterior: ___° interior: ___°

2 A 9-sided regular polygon
exterior: ___° interior: ___°

3 A 10-sided regular polygon
exterior: ___° interior: ___°

4 A 12-sided regular polygon
exterior: ___° interior: ___°

5 An 8-sided regular polygon
exterior: ___° interior: ___°

6 An 18-sided regular polygon
exterior: ___° interior: ___°

7 A 5-sided regular polygon
exterior: ___° interior: ___°

8 A 15-sided regular polygon
exterior: ___° interior: ___°

Today I scored ___ out of 8.

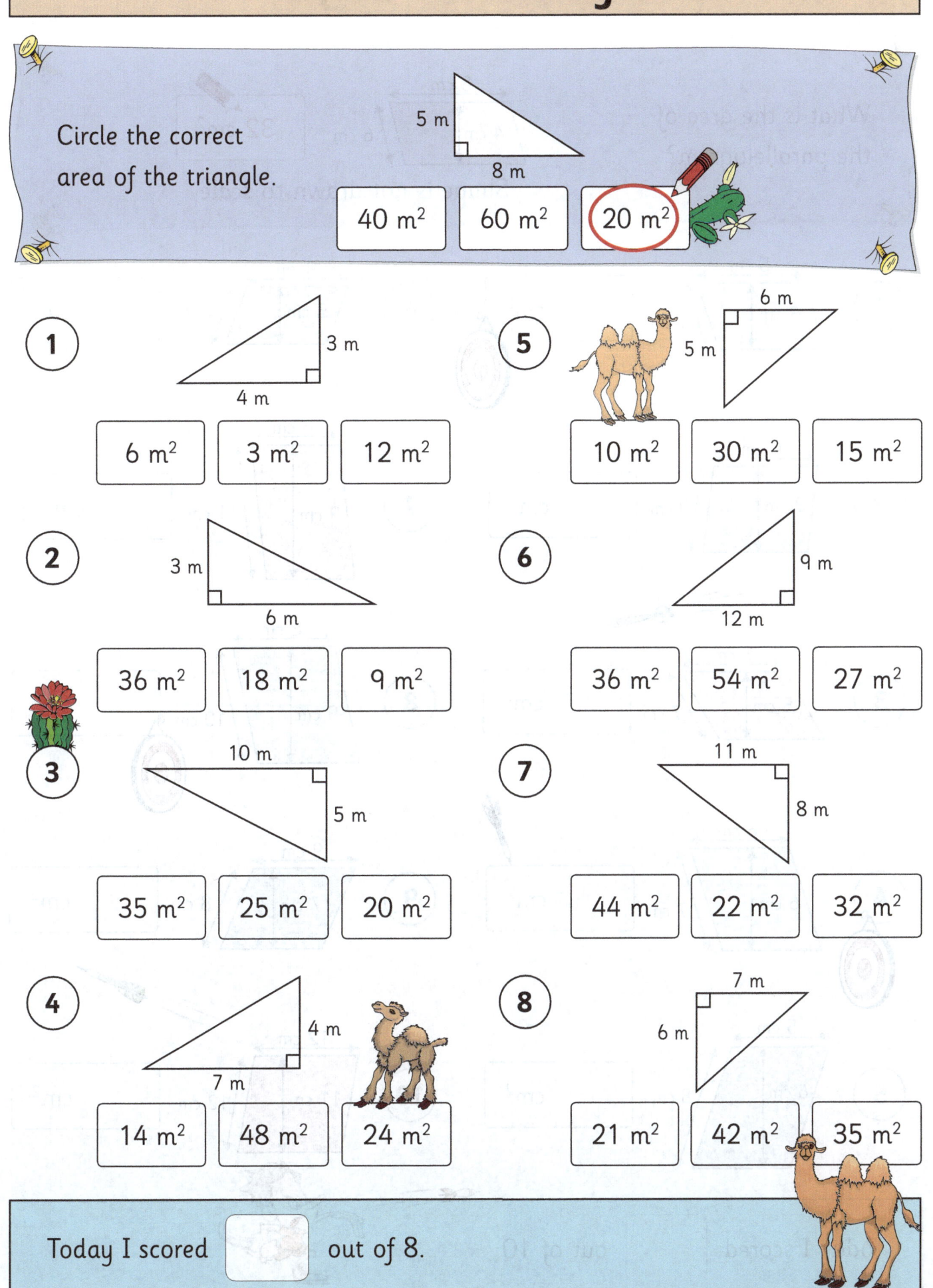

Week 11 — Day 2

What is the area of the parallelogram? (8 cm, 4 cm, 6 cm) → **32 cm²**

Shape is not drawn to scale

1. 5 cm, 3 cm, 4 cm → ___ cm²
2. 10 cm, 8 cm, 9 cm → ___ cm²
3. 8 cm, 5 cm, 7 cm → ___ cm²
4. 6 cm, 6 cm, 7 cm → ___ cm²
5. 5 cm, 6 cm, 8 cm → ___ cm²
6. 9 cm, 5 cm, 6 cm → ___ cm²
7. 6 cm, 9 cm, 11 cm → ___ cm²
8. 8 cm, 9 cm, 10 cm → ___ cm²
9. 9 cm, 7 cm, 8 cm → ___ cm²
10. 12 cm, 11 cm, 12 cm → ___ cm²

Today I scored ___ out of 10.

Week 11 — Day 3

A bowl weighs 75 g. What is the total mass of the bowl and food?

A bowl with 10 plums, each plum weighing 65 g. **725** g

1) A bowl with 10 apples, each apple weighing 87 g. _____ g

2) A bowl with 1000 raisins, each raisin weighing 0.52 g. _____ g

3) A bowl with 100 cherries, each cherry weighing 5.6 g. _____ g

4) A bowl with 10 oranges, each orange weighing 113 g. _____ g

5) A bowl with 100 figs, each fig weighing 40.7 g. _____ g

6) A bowl with 10 pears, each pear weighing 159 g. _____ g

7) A bowl with 1000 seeds, each seed weighing 0.315 g. _____ g

8) A bowl with 1000 nuts, each nut weighing 1.28 g. _____ g

9) A bowl with 100 grapes, each grape weighing 4.91 g. _____ g

10) A bowl with 100 berries, each berry weighing 6.24 g. _____ g

Today I scored _____ out of 10.

Week 11 — Day 4

The perimeter of the swimming pool is 60 m. Work out the area.

5 m

The area is 125 m².

1) 10 m — The area is ☐ m².

2) 15 m — The area is ☐ m².

3) 8 m — The area is ☐ m².

4) 6 m — The area is ☐ m².

5) 3 m — The area is ☐ m².

6) 7 m — The area is ☐ m².

7) 13 m — The area is ☐ m².

8) 12 m — The area is ☐ m².

Today I scored ☐ out of 8.

Week 11 — Day 5

How many more metres of the fence are needed? Give your answer as a mixed number in its simplest form.

The fence should be 8 m long.
David has built $4\frac{2}{5}$ m.
Stacy has built $\frac{3}{10}$ m.
They need $3\frac{3}{10}$ m more.

1 The fence should be 3 m long.
Grace has built $\frac{1}{3}$ m.
Ava has built $1\frac{1}{6}$ m.
They need $1\frac{1}{2}$ m more.

2 The fence should be 7 m long.
Zoe has built $3\frac{1}{4}$ m.
Noah has built $\frac{5}{12}$ m.
They need $3\frac{1}{3}$ m more.

3 The fence should be 5 m long.
Owen has built $1\frac{3}{5}$ m.
Ella has built $2\frac{1}{10}$ m.
They need $1\frac{3}{10}$ m more.

4 The fence should be 4 m long.
Maya has built $1\frac{3}{4}$ m.
Ryan has built $\frac{1}{6}$ m.
They need $2\frac{1}{12}$ m more.

5 The fence should be 6 m long.
Elijah has built $1\frac{1}{10}$ m.
Suki has built $2\frac{2}{3}$ m.
They need $2\frac{7}{30}$ m more.

6 The fence should be 9 m long.
Clara has built $3\frac{2}{3}$ m.
Ivan has built $2\frac{1}{8}$ m.
They need $3\frac{5}{24}$ m more.

Today I scored ☐ out of 6.

Week 12 — Day 1

What is the volume of the cuboid? 2 m, 4 m, 6 m — **48** m³

1. 5 m, 2 m, 1 m → ☐ m³
2. 3 m, 7 m, 3 m → ☐ m³
3. 4 m, 3 m, 5 m → ☐ m³
4. 11 m, 5 m, 2 m → ☐ m³
5. 9 m, 8 m, 10 m → ☐ m³
6. 2 m, 6 m, 7 m → ☐ m³

Today I scored ☐ out of 6.

Week 12 — Day 2

For the two numbers shown, write down all the common multiples that are less than 100.

6, 15 → 30, 60, 90

1) 25, 5

2) 4, 10

3) 15, 25

4) 9, 12

5) 12, 15

6) 6, 16

7) 12, 8

8) 6, 14

9) 9, 6

10) 14, 4

Today I scored ☐ out of 10.

Week 12 — Day 3

Which cuboid has the larger volume?

Cuboid A has sides of length 2 cm, 5 cm and 8 cm.
Cuboid B has sides of length 6 cm, 1 cm and 9 cm.

Cuboid **A**

1. Cuboid C has sides of length 1 cm, 8 cm and 7 cm.
   Cuboid D has sides of length 2 cm, 6 cm and 3 cm.
   Cuboid _____

2. Cuboid E has sides of length 3 cm, 4 cm and 6 cm.
   Cuboid F has sides of length 3 cm, 3 cm and 12 cm.
   Cuboid _____

3. Cuboid G has sides of length 10 cm, 2 cm and 5 cm.
   Cuboid H has sides of length 2 cm, 9 cm and 6 cm.
   Cuboid _____

4. Cuboid I has sides of length 6 cm, 10 cm and 3 cm.
   Cuboid J has sides of length 4 cm, 11 cm and 6 cm.
   Cuboid _____

5. Cuboid K has sides of length 3 cm, 5 cm and 7 cm.
   Cuboid L has sides of length 7 cm, 2 cm and 6 cm.
   Cuboid _____

6. Cuboid M has sides of length 8 cm, 7 cm and 3 cm.
   Cuboid N has sides of length 5 cm, 4 cm and 6 cm.
   Cuboid _____

7. Cuboid O has sides of length 5 cm, 8 cm and 5 cm.
   Cuboid P has sides of length 6 cm, 4 cm and 7 cm.
   Cuboid _____

8. Cuboid Q has sides of length 2 cm, 12 cm and 6 cm.
   Cuboid R has sides of length 3 cm, 6 cm and 9 cm.
   Cuboid _____

Today I scored _____ out of 8.

Week 12 — Day 4

Round the number of items in each box to the nearest 10 and round the number of boxes to the nearest hundred. Use these numbers to estimate the total number of items.

Plates come in boxes of 16. There are 1302 boxes.

26 000

1. Pans come in boxes of 24. There are 2103 boxes.

2. Shirts come in boxes of 12. There are 1496 boxes.

3. Mats come in boxes of 18. There are 3747 boxes.

4. Flasks come in boxes of 27. There are 2441 boxes.

5. Forks come in boxes of 21. There are 1714 boxes.

6. Hats come in boxes of 33. There are 2251 boxes.

7. Mugs come in boxes of 28. There are 3127 boxes.

8. Trays come in boxes of 42. There are 2658 boxes.

Today I scored ⬜ out of 8.

Week 12 — Day 5

Circle the largest fraction. $\frac{5}{4}$ $\frac{7}{6}$ $\boxed{\frac{5}{3}}$

1) $\frac{3}{2}$ $\frac{7}{4}$ $\frac{11}{8}$

2) $\frac{11}{10}$ $\frac{7}{6}$ $\frac{6}{5}$

3) $\frac{5}{6}$ $\frac{2}{3}$ $\frac{5}{9}$

4) $\frac{11}{6}$ $\frac{9}{4}$ $\frac{8}{3}$

5) $\frac{11}{8}$ $\frac{5}{4}$ $\frac{11}{10}$

6) $\frac{5}{4}$ $\frac{7}{5}$ $\frac{9}{8}$

7) $\frac{5}{2}$ $\frac{13}{6}$ $\frac{9}{4}$

8) $\frac{8}{3}$ $\frac{7}{4}$ $\frac{5}{2}$

9) $\frac{7}{12}$ $\frac{5}{8}$ $\frac{2}{3}$

10) $\frac{9}{5}$ $\frac{11}{6}$ $\frac{5}{3}$

11) $\frac{7}{9}$ $\frac{2}{3}$ $\frac{3}{4}$

12) $\frac{5}{8}$ $\frac{7}{9}$ $\frac{11}{12}$

Today I scored ☐ out of 12.

Answers

Week 1 — Day 1
1. 56 cm
2. 70 cm
3. 59 cm
4. 60 cm
5. 47 cm
6. 69 cm
7. 91 cm
8. 77 cm
9. 105 cm
10. 93 cm
11. 92 cm
12. 116 cm

Week 1 — Day 2
1. $\frac{2}{15}$
2. $\frac{1}{6}$
3. $\frac{1}{4}$
4. $\frac{1}{10}$
5. $\frac{15}{44}$
6. $\frac{9}{35}$
7. $\frac{1}{8}$
8. $\frac{21}{32}$
9. $\frac{2}{5}$
10. $\frac{5}{24}$
11. $\frac{2}{5}$
12. $\frac{1}{5}$

Week 1 — Day 3
1. 27 859
2. 215 934
3. 173 484
4. 333 288
5. 147 420
6. 507 360

Week 1 — Day 4
1. 5 °C
2. 12 °C
3. 7 °C
4. 10 °C
5. 15 °C
6. 20 °C

Week 1 — Day 5
1. Yes
2. Yes
3. No
4. Yes
5. No
6. Yes
7. No
8. No
9. Yes
10. No
11. Yes
12. Yes

Week 2 — Day 1
1. 0.125
2. 0.18
3. 0.875
4. 0.35
5. 0.65
6. 0.26
7. 0.95
8. 0.74
9. 0.85
10. 0.66
11. 0.625
12. 0.82

Week 2 — Day 2
1. 24.1
2. 211.3
3. 461.2
4. 82.8
5. 61.1
6. 46.6
7. 115.64
8. 53.35
9. 104.2
10. 75.75
11. 97.65
12. 128.05

Week 2 — Day 3
1. Yes
2. Yes
3. No
4. No
5. Yes
6. Yes
7. No
8. Yes
9. Yes
10. No

Week 2 — Day 4
1. £9.50
2. £6.50
3. £9.04
4. £13.35
5. £11.28
6. £5.12
7. £2.08
8. £5.97

Week 2 — Day 5
1. E.g.
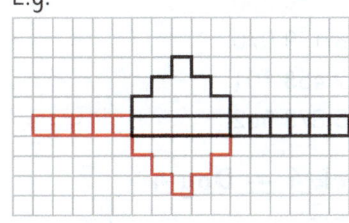
2. E.g.
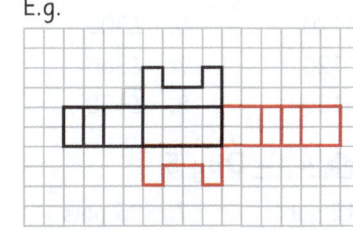
3. E.g.
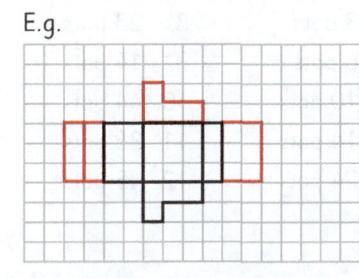

4. E.g
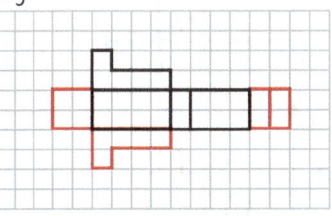

5. E.g
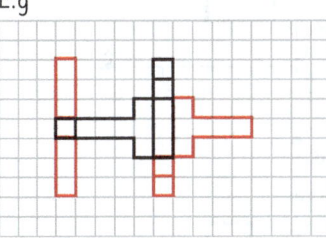

Week 3 — Day 1
1.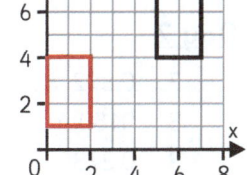
2.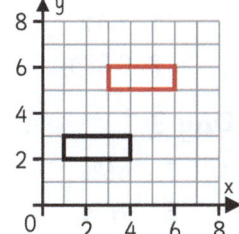
3.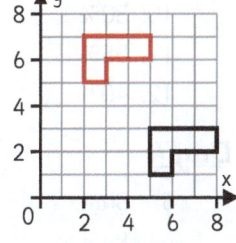
4.

5.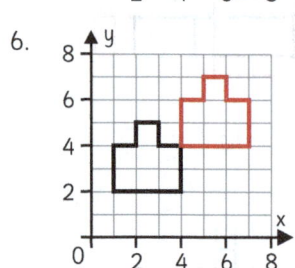

6.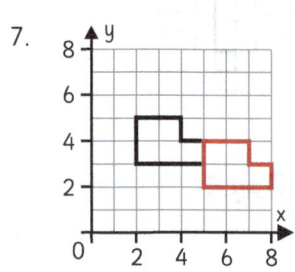

7.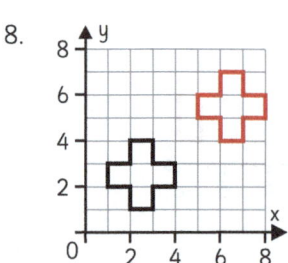

8.

Week 3 — Day 2
1. 235
2. 629
3. 18.3
4. 542
5. 2.79
6. 45.7
7. 0.872
8. 9150
9. 0.373
10. 783
11. 7.41
12. 0.834

Week 3 — Day 3
1. 13%
2. 59%
3. 50%
4. 70%
5. 20%
6. 25%
7. 66%
8. 76%
9. 44%
10. 80%
11. 55%
12. 40%

Week 3 — Day 4
1. Levi
2. Adam
3. Cali
4. Lana
5. Stan
6. Rafe
7. Priti
8. Lee

Week 3 — Day 5
1. Amy
2. Raj
3. Hina
4. Liam
5. Liz
6. Jim
7. Kyle
8. Mia

Week 4 — Day 1
1. 3
2. 5
3. 7
4. 8
5. 6
6. 12
7. 12
8. 9
9. 8
10. 16
11. 8
12. 7

Week 4 — Day 2
1. lines of symmetry **4** acute angles **0**
2. lines of symmetry **2** acute angles **0**
3. lines of symmetry **3** acute angles **3**
4. lines of symmetry **0** acute angles **2**
5. lines of symmetry **5** acute angles **0**
6. lines of symmetry **2** acute angles **2**
7. lines of symmetry **6** acute angles **0**
8. lines of symmetry **7** acute angles **0**

Week 4 — Day 3
1. 690 000
2. 561 000
3. 9 436 200
4. 8 139 070
5. 2 453 101
6. 5 878 562

Week 4 — Day 4
1. £65
2. £120
3. £120
4. £180
5. £450
6. £300
7. £360
8. £120

Week 4 — Day 5
1. 12 pots
2. 8 pots
3. 6 pots
4. 10 pots
5. 14 pots
6. 24 pots
7. 35 pots
8. 20 pots
9. 14 pots
10. 44 pots
11. 36 pots
12. 45 pots

Week 5 — Day 1
1. 3 pigs
2. 6 pigs
3. 5 pigs
4. 30 pigs
5. 36 pigs
6. 9 pigs
7. 60 pigs
8. 23 pigs
9. 100 pigs
10. 70 pigs
11. 600 pigs
12. 450 pigs

Week 5 — Day 2
1. 24 m
2. 22 m
3. 35 m
4. 32 m
5. 30 m
6. 72 m
7. 48 m
8. 200 m
9. 57 m
10. 98 m

Week 5 — Day 3
1. 21
2. 8
3. 35
4. 42
5. 20
6. 77
7. 40
8. 105
9. 490
10. 50

Week 5 — Day 4
1. 3
2. 5
3. 4
4. 12
5. 3
6. 9
7. 6
8. 10

Week 5 — Day 5
1. Yes
2. No
3. Yes
4. Yes
5. Yes
6. No
7. No
8. Yes

Week 6 — Day 1
1. add 5
2. add 7
3. subtract 4
4. add 9
5. subtract 30
6. subtract 12
7. add 13
8. subtract 6
9. subtract 20
10. add 35
11. subtract 17
12. add 18

Week 6 — Day 2
1. <
2. <
3. =
4. >
5. <
6. >
7. =

Week 6 — Day 3

1. 10, 12, 14
2. 9, 14, 19
3. 1, 5, 9
4. 15, 23, 31
5. 2, 8, 14
6. 20, 29, 38
7. 3, 15, 27
8. −2, 2, 6
9. −9, −2, 5
10. −7, −2, 3
11. −5, 7, 19
12. −10, −2, 6

Week 6 — Day 4

1. £220
2. £270
3. £355
4. £905
5. £662
6. £198.50

Week 6 — Day 5

1. Jack
2. Joyce
3. John
4. Ming
5. Albert
6. Farhad

Week 7 — Day 1

1. 8 753 210
2. 2 456 798
3. 8 875 423
4. 8 655 434
5. 1 224 598
6. 1 234 483
7. 4 466 883
8. 9 884 207

Week 7 — Day 2

1. ■ = 1, ■ = 2, ○ = 8, ○ = 2
2. ■ = 1, ■ = 2, ■ = 3, ○ = 7, ○ = 4, ○ = 1
3. ■ = 1, ■ = 2, ■ = 3, ○ = 16, ○ = 9, ○ = 2
4. ■ = 1, ■ = 2, ○ = 10, ○ = 2
5. ■ = 2, ■ = 5, ■ = 10, ○ = 3, ○ = 6, ○ = 7
6. ■ = 1, ■ = 3, ■ = 7, ○ = 19, ○ = 5, ○ = 1

Week 7 — Day 3

1. 10
2. 80
3. 36
4. 25
5. 22
6. 21
7. 24
8. 20

Week 7 — Day 4

1. $3x = 15$ and $x = 5$
2. $8x = 24$ and $x = 3$
3. $7x = 49$ and $x = 7$
4. $6x - 6 = 18$ and $x = 4$
5. $2x - 3 = 13$ and $x = 8$
6. $9x + 7 = 34$ and $x = 3$
7. $4x + 9 = 45$ and $x = 9$
8. $8x - 5 = 51$ and $x = 7$

Week 7 — Day 5

1. A = 7, B = 1
2. A = 5, B = 3
3. A = 3, B = 9
4. A = 6, B = 4
5. A = 8, B = 2
6. A = 1, B = 5
7. A = 8, B = 6
8. A = 9, B = 6

Week 8 — Day 1

1. 3.75
2. 27.36
3. 13.88
4. 35.56
5. 35.68
6. 62.73
7. 30.87
8. 16.38
9. 60.34
10. 89.91
11. 46.32
12. 77.04

Week 8 — Day 2

(not drawn full size)

1. E.g.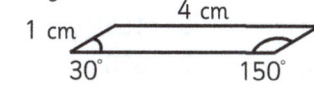
2. E.g.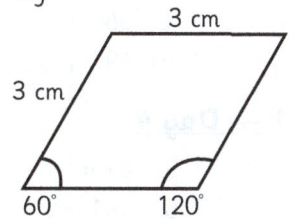
3. E.g.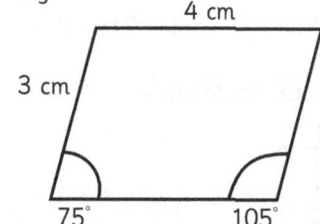

4. E.g.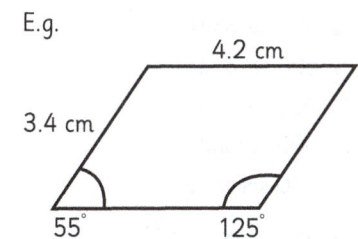

5. E.g.

Week 8 — Day 3

1. 824 m
2. 30.3 cm
3. 831 mm
4. 120.6 cm
5. 2.237 cm
6. 0.337 km
7. 2.492 cm
8. 795 m
9. 0.971 m
10. 1.741 km

Week 8 — Day 4

1. Rani
2. Toby
3. Rani
4. Toby
5. Rani
6. Rani
7. Toby
8. Rani
9. Toby
10. Toby

Week 8 — Day 5

1. 10 cm
2. 20 cm
3. 74 cm
4. 110 cm
5. 95 cm
6. 122 cm

Week 9 — Day 1

1. $\frac{9}{6}$ and $\frac{3}{2}$
2. $\frac{4}{5}$ and $\frac{8}{10}$
3. $\frac{12}{16}$ and $\frac{3}{4}$
4. $\frac{13}{12}$ and $\frac{26}{24}$
5. $\frac{11}{4}$ and $\frac{22}{8}$
6. $5\frac{4}{5}$ and $\frac{58}{10}$
7. $4\frac{1}{2}$ and $\frac{36}{8}$
8. $2\frac{2}{5}$ and $2\frac{4}{10}$
9. $\frac{9}{6}$ and $\frac{12}{8}$
10. $\frac{7}{2}$ and $3\frac{5}{10}$

Week 9 — Day 2

1. 2.63 kg
2. 3.6 kg
3. 3.23 kg
4. 6.87 kg
5. 2.337 kg
6. 7.721 kg
7. 1.384 kg
8. 4.77 kg

Week 9 — Day 3
1. 1980 seconds
2. 1620 seconds
3. 3060 seconds
4. 1440 seconds
5. 10 800 seconds
6. 32 400 seconds
7. 57 600 seconds
8. 30 000 seconds
9. 15 000 seconds
10. 19 800 seconds

Week 9 — Day 4
1. 1100 ml
2. 2200 ml
3. 1110 ml
4. 520 ml
5. 815 ml
6. 2705 ml
7. 7220 ml
8. 1690 ml

Week 9 — Day 5
1. 5600
2. 1680
3. 2940
4. 1260
5. 4165
6. 8372
7. 25 284
8. 38 024

Week 10 — Day 1
1. x = 60°, y = 110°
2. x = 80°, y = 50°
3. x = 110°, y = 115°
4. x = 45°, y = 95°
5. x = 77°, y = 92°
6. x = 84°, y = 71°
7. x = 108°, y = 78°
8. x = 73°, y = 113°

Week 10 — Day 2
1. 160°
2. 120°
3. 105°
4. 85°
5. 54°
6. 58°
7. 73°
8. 116°

Week 10 — Day 3
1. 41 + 10 ÷ 2 = 46
2. 8 × (9 − 6) = 24
3. 54 + 6 ÷ 2 = 57
4. 28 − 8 ÷ 4 = 26
5. 24 − 8 ÷ 2 = 20
6. 66 − 12 ÷ 4 = 63
7. 27 − 4 × 3 = 15
8. 36 ÷ (7 − 4) = 12
9. 42 ÷ (4 + 2) = 7
10. 38 + 4 × 6 = 62
11. 12 × (5 + 3) = 96
12. 47 + 7 × 11 = 124

Week 10 — Day 4
1. 90°
2. 65°
3. 120°
4. 50°
5. 135°
6. 70°
7. 60°
8. 80°
9. 35°
10. 101°

Week 10 — Day 5
1. exterior = 90°, interior = 90°
2. exterior = 40°, interior = 140°
3. exterior = 36°, interior = 144°
4. exterior = 30°, interior = 150°
5. exterior = 45°, interior = 135°
6. exterior = 20°, interior = 160°
7. exterior = 72°, interior = 108°
8. exterior = 24°, interior = 156°

Week 11 — Day 1
1. 6 m²
2. 9 m²
3. 25 m²
4. 14 m²
5. 15 m²
6. 54 m²
7. 44 m²
8. 21 m²

Week 11 — Day 2
1. 15 cm²
2. 80 cm²
3. 40 cm²
4. 36 cm²
5. 30 cm²
6. 45 cm²
7. 54 cm²
8. 72 cm²
9. 63 cm²
10. 132 cm²

Week 11 — Day 3
1. 945 g
2. 595 g
3. 635 g
4. 1205 g
5. 4145 g
6. 1665 g
7. 390 g
8. 1355 g
9. 566 g
10. 699 g

Week 11 — Day 4
1. 200 m²
2. 225 m²
3. 176 m²
4. 144 m²
5. 81 m²
6. 161 m²
7. 221 m²
8. 216 m²

Week 11 — Day 5
1. $1\frac{1}{2}$ m
2. $3\frac{1}{3}$ m
3. $1\frac{3}{10}$ m
4. $2\frac{1}{12}$ m
5. $2\frac{7}{30}$ m
6. $3\frac{5}{24}$ m

Week 12 — Day 1
1. 10 m³
2. 63 m³
3. 60 m³
4. 110 m³
5. 720 m³
6. 84 m³

Week 12 — Day 2
1. 25, 50, 75
2. 20, 40, 60, 80
3. 75
4. 36, 72
5. 60
6. 48, 96
7. 24, 48, 72, 96
8. 42, 84
9. 18, 36, 54, 72, 90
10. 28, 56, 84

Week 12 — Day 3
1. Cuboid C
2. Cuboid F
3. Cuboid H
4. Cuboid J
5. Cuboid K
6. Cuboid M
7. Cuboid O
8. Cuboid R

Week 12 — Day 4
1. 42 000
2. 15 000
3. 74 000
4. 72 000
5. 34 000
6. 69 000
7. 93 000
8. 108 000

Week 12 — Day 5
1. $\frac{7}{4}$
2. $\frac{6}{5}$
3. $\frac{5}{6}$
4. $\frac{8}{3}$
5. $\frac{11}{8}$
6. $\frac{7}{5}$
7. $\frac{5}{2}$
8. $\frac{8}{3}$
9. $\frac{2}{3}$
10. $\frac{11}{6}$
11. $\frac{7}{9}$
12. $\frac{11}{12}$

Answers